LEARNING TO FAIL

CASE STUDIES OF STUDENTS AT RISK

Phi Delta Kappa
Maynard R. Bemis Center
for Evaluation, Development, and Research
Bloomington, Indiana

Cover design by
VICTORIA VOELKER

Edited by
DEBORAH BURNETT STROTHER

Photographs by
DAVID M. GROSSMAN,
JEFFREY HIGH,
and
VICTORIA VOELKER

*(The photographs in this book are for graphic
purposes only. They do not depict the subjects
portrayed in the case studies.)*

Library of Congress Catalog Card Number 91-62424
ISBN 0-87367-728-5
Copyright © 1991 Phi Delta Kappa

Oh, narrow, blind, and witless preachers!
  Do we expect the "ragged" band
To be among Earth's perfect creatures,
  While we refuse the helping hand?

To work, to work! with hope and joy,
  Let us be doing what we can;
Better build schoolrooms for "the boy,"
  Than cells and gibbets for "the man."

"A Song for the Ragged Schools"
Poems by Eliza Cook, 1866

PROJECT DIRECTORS

Jack Frymier
Senior Fellow
Phi Delta Kappa

Neville Robertson
Director
Phi Delta Kappa Center for the
Dissemination of Innovative Programs

Larry Barber
Director
Phi Delta Kappa Center for
Evaluation, Development, Research

RESEARCH COORDINATORS
Phi Delta Kappa Chapter-Based Research Project

Gary Dill
Chapter 0128
St. Cloud State University
St. Cloud, Minnesota

Joanne Herbert
Chapter 0026
University of Virginia
Charlottesville, Virginia

Joe Klingstedt
Chapter 0171
University of Texas, El Paso
El Paso, Texas

Delwyn L. Harnisch
Chapter 0016
University of Illinois at
  Urbana-Champaign
Champaign, Illinois

Nedra Sears
Chapter 1309
East Central University
Ada, Oklahoma

Cynthia K. Terres
Chapter 1204
Farthest North Alaska
Fairbanks, Alaska

Alice Woods
Chapter 1471
Florida Southern College
University of South Florida
Lakeland, Florida

Dennis Zuelke
Chapter 0152
Univ. of Wisconsin, Superior
Superior, Wisconsin

vi

AUTHORS OF CASE STUDIES
Phi Delta Kappa Chapter-Based Research Project

Delwyn L. Harnisch
Director, Educational Testing,
  Research, and Service
University of Illinois at
  Urbana-Champaign
Champaign, Illinois

Robin Hasslen
Instructor
St. Cloud State University
St. Cloud, Minnesota

Steve Larson (deceased)
Maple School District
Maple, Wisconsin

Linda Mabry
Spencer Fellow
University of Illinois
Urbana-Champaign, Illinois

Betty J. McKinny
Teacher
Fairbanks School District
Fairbanks, Alaska

Dennis Bixler-Márquez
Director, Chicano Studies
University of Texas at El Paso
El Paso, Texas

Mara Reid and
Susan Van Leuven
Division of Student Services
Leon County Schools
Tallahassee, Florida

Nedra Sears
Associate Professor
East Central University
Ada, Oklahoma

Milagros M. Seda
Elementary and Secondary
  Studies
University of Texas at El Paso
El Paso, Texas

Linda Trice
Principal
Oklahoma School for the Deaf
Sulphur, Oklahoma

John Vaughn
Assistant Professor
Special Education
East Central University
Ada, Oklahoma

Laqueta Vaughn
Special Education Program
Specialist, Pre K-12
McAlester Public Schools
McAlester, Oklahoma

Eleanor Vernon Wilson
Curry School of Education
University of Virginia
Charlottesville, Virginia

Alice Woods
Adjunct Professor
Florida Southern College
University of South Florida
Lakeland, Florida

CONTENTS

PREFACE

This book is about individual children who are at risk in America today. Each chapter is a case study of one student who was identified by a teacher or teachers as being seriously at risk and then described by a researcher trying to understand risk and how risk manifests itself in the life and mind of that particular child.

Each child is different. We all know that, of course, but professionals and institutions often overlook differences and focus on the similarities that exist among young people. For example, young people may share a common blood type or ethnic background. They may speak a common language or share a particular religious upbringing. Despite these similarities, every human being is unique. Genetically, no two people in the world are alike, except identical twins. Experientially we are all unique. No two people have the same experiences — even identical twins — thus uniqueness and difference are an important part of life itself.

If we ask which aspects of a student's existence are most affected by education, the answer seems clear. Those things that one person shares with other people are important, but is the differences among students that make differences in teaching obligatory and differences in learning routine.

It is in the area of individuality — uniqueness — that education and educators can make a difference. These case studies, therefore, are important as a basis for learning more about learning in school.

The Phi Delta Kappa Study of Students At Risk was an attempt to answer four questions through research:

1. Who is at risk?
2. What about them puts them at risk?
3. What are the schools doing to help those students?
4. How effective are those efforts?

The project was initiated with a general definition of risk by assuming that students at risk are young people who are likely to fail at school or fail at life. A child who gets straight Fs on his or her report card is at risk of dropping out of school. Likewise, a young person who is contemplating or has attempted suicide is seriously at risk.

Information was collected about 49,000 students and almost 10,000 teachers in more than 275 schools in 85 communities across the country in an effort to answer the questions set forth above. In addition, researchers conducted case studies of 65 young people to illustrate the reality and amplify the uniqueness of what it means to be at risk in diverse ways. Eleven of those case studies have been selected for publication.

Each case study was prepared by a researcher in the local area in which the student lived. We gave credit to the authors, but in the spirit of confidentiality decided not to make the direct link by indicating which case study was prepared by whom — since knowledge of the authors' locations might make identification of the student possible. It certainly would make it more probable. Our primary concern was to protect the children whose lives are described.

Each of the young people described here is very much at risk, and the case studies highlight each child's risk in dramatic ways.

Neville Robertson
Jack Frymier

INTRODUCTION

The case studies reported in this book are vivid snapshots of 11 children who attended public schools in America during the 1980s. Their stories are unique. Each is set against a different landscape with a different home situation and different societal pressures and demands. Their stories also are similar. Many of the problems the 11 children faced are the same, as are many of their solutions. Most of them learned about failing from an early age.

Today, the picture of American childhood is different from that of earlier generations. While poverty is not a new stress for children, the growing numbers of poor children are alarming. So, too, are numbers of children with handicaps (many due to the substance abuse of their mothers), inadequate preventive health, and lack of adequate parenting.

- In 1989, twenty-three percent (23%) of America's children age 0-5 were below the federal poverty line according to the Census Bureau. Because poverty is calculated on the ability of parents to buy food, and federal nutrition programs are limited, most of the children in this cohort are poor and subject to malnutrition.
- Almost one in four children born in the U.S. today is born out of wedlock. . . . Fifteen million children in America are being raised by a single parent. Almost half of these children are being raised in poverty. . . .
- Twenty percent (20%) of America's children have not been vaccinated against polio; in California *half* of the children have not received immunization shots for basic childhood diseases.
- Eleven percent (11%) of America's students are enrolled in classes for the handicapped.

Demographics for Education Newsletter
vol. 1, no. 3 (March 1990)
Center for Demographic Policy

A list compiled by the Children's Defense Fund, puts the picture of today's child into sharper focus.

- Every 35 seconds an infant is born into poverty.
- Every 14 minutes an infant dies in the first year of life.
- Every night 100,000 children go to sleep without homes.
- Every week in 1990, 327 children got measles, which could have been prevented by adequate immunizations.
- Every month at least 56,000 children are abused.
- Every 14 hours a child younger than 5 is murdered.
- Every 2 seconds of the school day a public school student is suspended.
- Every 4 seconds of the school day a public school student is corporally punished.
- Every 10 seconds of the school day a student drops out of school.

Children's Defense Fund
The State of America's Children 1991, p. 5

Regardless of who takes the picture, it is clear that our children are under increasing stress. Dropout rates are high and academic achievement low. Poverty, violence, drugs, teen pregnancy, and AIDS are common concerns in many school districts, and educators are applying the label at-risk to more and more of their students.

Parents were once a major influence in the lives of their children. They are less so today. Television, a window to the world and to new attitudes, is everywhere. A single parent often heads the household or both parents work. Grandparents live farther away or divorce has separated them from their grandchildren. Today, as children need adults more than ever to help combat the growing lists of stresses, they are less available. The stresses are so great in some cases that children find it difficult to focus on classwork. This problem often is further complicated by irrelevant or outdated curricula.

At a time when patriotism is strong in America, our concern for each other appears weak. We may have won a war in Saudi Arabia, but we are losing the wars on poverty, drugs, and illiteracy in our own country. Even as we boast of our country's strengths, we blame each other for society's shortcomings. We have blamed schools, in particular, for the problems of students. For the past eight years Americans have been speaking and writing about educators and educational systems as if the education field was an isolated segment of  our society, solely responsible for how children fare both inside and outside schools.

People who work in schools often do feel isolated. Theirs is a unique culture, but it reflects the larger culture it serves — the values and mores, as well as current subjects of interest. It follows, therefore, that if our students are at risk, our culture — all of us — must also be at risk.

In an interview with Bill Moyers, veteran teacher Mike Rose revealed his experiences as an at-risk child of the 1960s — his poverty, average work in elementary school, and accidental placement in the vocational track during his first two years of high school. "What's interesting to me about that experience is not that an unusual thing happened, but that it shows how arbitrary placement in 'fast track' and 'slow track' can be. It also shows how students placed in the slow track live down to the expectations of their classrooms. And finally, it suggests to me that for parents who are not socialized into that whole way of thinking about education, it's very easy not to realize that something is amiss."[1] Rose said that the raw power of education is so strong that children often feel left out. These feelings are manifest in a variety of ways according to Rose — students are sullen and silent, make lots of noise, become the class clown, get stoned on drugs, or are absent a lot — all ways to defend themselves against the feeling of not belonging. Unfortunately, they also are ways of failing.

Author Susan Gordon recently wrote, "The United States is experiencing an extreme crisis in caring. As a society we cannot seem to muster the political will to care for the most precious things we produce — other human beings."[2] The indicators of our crisis, she says, are our homeless families, our high infant mortality rate, and the large numbers of our citizens and their children who are living in poverty, with inadequate or no health insurance. Our education system is a shambles, and recent political decisions have discouraged care giving for the young and the old. Our country's negative attitude toward caring discourages people from entering the caring professions such as teaching and nursing, and even clouds personal relations between men and women. Americans, says Ms. Gordon, are emotionally deprived: "We have children other people care for, friends we have no time to socialize with, spouses about whom we complain but with whom we have no time to structure to create more fulfilling relationships." A National Care Agenda, she suggests, could end the crisis.

The details of her program are controversial, particularly for those people opposed to our current welfare system. Yet her sentiments seem appropriate in this at-risk age. If Americans can renew their patriotism, why can't we care for fellow Americans who need help?

Schools provide the right conditions and opportunities to implement an agenda of caring, whether in a classroom, school, or the whole district, suggests Alphie Kohn in a recent Kappan article.[3] He proposed the idea of teaching children to internalize the value of community, and not just the good values in a community.

Schools are a part of our culture and an important part of each community. They do not exist in isolation and many educators are suggesting we would all benefit if schools filled an expanded roll. Larry Barber, director of Phi Delta Kappa's Center for Evaluation, Development, and Research, predicted, "We can no longer afford to operate independently. The schools are going to have to start taking a leadership role in coordinating the home and all other social agencies, including the courts, the police, the social service agencies, child welfare, to be able to save these kids."[4]

In her book *Within Our Reach: Breaking the Cycle of Disadvantage*, Lisbeth Schorr details places in America where schools are providing superb health, education, and social services to children. If these services "were more widely available," she predicts, "fewer children would come into adulthood unschooled and unskilled, committing violent crimes, and bearing children as unmarried teenagers. Fewer of today's vulnerable children would tomorrow swell the welfare rolls and the prisons. Many more would grow into responsible and productive adults, able to form stable families and contributing to, rather than depleting, America's prosperity and sense of community."[5]

Stories about children at risk, like those in Schorr's book and in this monograph, provide shocking examples of the lack of coordinated services available to children at risk within our society. They also provide information about how children can be helped to overcome their problems and eventually become productive members of their communities.

This book resulted from the work of Phi Delta Kappa (PDK) members who themselves form a strong community. While the information they gathered was valuable, an important outcome of the process for those educators and their institutions was involvement in the process itself. Collaborating with one another and working within the PDK community was a valuable experience for those volunteers. Working together also gave participants a chance to share stories, discuss outcomes, and compare insights.

THE STUDY

The Design

Jack Frymier, senior fellow of PDK International Headquarters and chairman of the coordinating committee of the PDK Chapter-Based Research Project, worked with committee members to develop a research design to address the issue of students at risk. The committee developed an innovative research methodology — simultaneous replication — and involved the community of PDK chapter members to carry out the research. Researchers in 85 communities studied children at risk. All participants used the same definitions, procedures, and instruments. Project coordinators collected and analyzed their data according to the same timeline and techniques.

Details of the study are included in the monograph *A Study of Students at Risk: Collaborating to Do Research*, by Jack Frymier. Details about the methodology are included in the article "Simultaneous Replication: A Technique for Large-Scale Research" by Jack Frymier, Larry Barber, Bruce Gansneder, and Neville Robertson (*Phi Delta Kappan*, November 1989).

The Tasks

The PDK Chapter-Based Research Project researchers had to accomplish four tasks.

1. Select one child in grade _____ (they were randomly assigned a level — elementary, junior high, or high school — and instructed to "select the one student at the grade level specified who, in your judgment, is most seriously at risk."
2. Prepare a cumulative folder for that one child.
3. Produce two videotapes related to that child [instructions detailed what tapes should focus on, scenes and interviews to include, and additional technical information about equipment and filming conditions].
4. Prepare a narrative description of that child.[6]

Subjects were told to secure permissions from the student and his or her parent(s) and to "indicate to the parents that all evidence suggests the student is having difficulty at school, and you hope to learn about the student so you can help that youngster learn more effectively."[7]

Participants were to be kept anonymous. "The intent is for you to bring together a complete set of information for this particular student . . . such as would typically be available and helpful to teachers and other professionals who might work with the student."[8]

Project designers did not specify methodology for the case studies, and researchers' techniques varied from naturalistic inquiry to more traditional scientific methodological procedures. The time researchers spent with their subjects also varied, as did the environments and conditions in which the interviews were held. Researchers visited one child on death row, where during the interview he sat handcuffed and under surveillance by prison staff. He had been sentenced to die for a murder he committed at age 15. Other interviews took place in homes, schools, and local teen hangouts.

Reflections

Few participants were unaffected by the research. They spent much time with their subjects and developed great insight into their lives. Some felt frightened as they entered prisons or searched out trailer homes tucked away deep in the countryside. Others were shocked and saddened by conditions in the child's life. Occasionally their deep feelings are evident in the case studies they wrote. In follow-up interviews, many researchers wanted to talk at length about their subjects. They also wanted to talk about how the study had changed their views of education, the course of their own work, and even their lives. One researcher said she now challenged the standard definition of multicultural. "The culture of poor or educationally deprived students is distinct," she said, "with language and value standards that depart significantly from middle-class culture."[9] "Normal" behavior for poor children, she said, is different from that of middle- or upper-class

Victoria Voelker

children. To fail to recognize this enlarged definition of multicultural, she concluded, places new teachers at a disadvantage when working with such families.

THE CASE STUDIES

The children in this book have problems. Their stories are alarming; a few haunting. Some are sad, others will provoke anger. And some might even remind you of your own school days. All the stories will raise more questions than they answer.

The book contains 11 stories about children who were deemed "at risk" by their teachers, counselors, or principals. Although the children were labeled at risk and provided with assistance from their schools, the help was often scattered among different agencies and uncoordinated. Several researchers discovered that the needs of their subjects were met by few teachers. One researcher estimated that of her subject's six teachers only one identified a specific need and made allowances in teaching techniques.

As you read about the children's lives, you may notice that positive comments about the students usually came from those teachers the students liked and who liked them. The teacher-student match appeared very important. You also may notice the ways the schools responded to these children and how they coped with those responses. Several of the children found out how to get out of a school they hated. As one child we call Roach put it, "I found out that I didn't have to take spankings. I could leave or get suspended." The schools were unable to teach Roach how to make it and so he found ways on his own to avoid his problems at an early age. He avoided trouble with school work by not going to school. He felt good about himself by using drugs and alcohol. He found role models — brothers and older friends who drank and used drugs. He became financially independent by robbing people. He solved a serious family problem by killing the person causing the trouble. And he learned to read — on death row.[10] Roach got an education. But not the one his teachers and parents thought they were providing.

HOW TO USE THIS BOOK

Educators can learn much about today's children from reading these case studies. Listen to the children and find out what problems they face, how the schools deal with them, and the results of that intervention.

Readers may notice similarities among the children, which will provoke stimulating comparisons and contrasts for discussion. However, each child is unique. All children are unique and bring to schools very different sets of needs.

The Center for Evaluation, Development, and Research hopes that this book will help educators and all people working with today's children develop a greater sensitivity to their problems, compassion for their "solutions" to them, and motivation to help find ways to ensure that all children get the education society wants them to have.   -DBS

1. Bill Moyers, *A World of Ideas* (New York: Doubleday, 1990), p. 219.
2. Susan Gordon, "A National Care Agenda," *Atlantic Monthly*, January 1991, p. 64.
3. Alphie Kohn, "Caring Kids: The Role of the Schools," *Phi Delta Kappan*, March 1991, p. 501.
4. Perspectives on Education 8 Series, "Students at Risk: A Case in Point," PDK Media Presentation (Bloomington, Ind.: 1990).
5. Lisbeth B. Schorr, *Within Our Reach: Breaking the Cycle of Disadvantage* (New York: Doubleday, 1988), p. xxvii.

6. Jack Frymier, Larry Barber, Ruben Carriedo, William Denton, Bruce Gansneder, Sharon Johnson-Lewis, Neville Robertson, *Manual of Instructions for A Study of Students at Risk* (Bloomington, Ind.: Phi Delta Kappa, 1988).

7. Ibid.

8. Ibid.

9. Nedra C. Sears, Kathleen Lehman, Laqueta Vaughn, John Vaughn, and Linda Trice, "A Case for Case Studies of At-Risk Students," paper presented at Oklahoma Educational Research Symposium 5, April 7, 1989.

10. Ibid.

NICOLE, SEEKING ATTENTION

Algebra Class, 8:00 a.m.

A few minutes after algebra class began, a sullen-looking girl entered the room. The teacher, who had finished distributing last week's graded quizzes, silently handed Nicole hers. She looked at the grade, rolled her eyes upward, and slumped into a seat at the back of the first row. Hanging a denim jacket across the seat, she revealed a blue and white striped oxford shirt emblazoned with beer patches. Despite the cold Midwestern January, she wore tennis shoes without laces and without socks.

"On Thursday, we'll have the final quiz before semester exams," the teacher announced. "So pay attention as we go over the formulas." He filled the blackboard with equations, explaining each. Twenty-seven sophomores sat silently. The class was half girls and half boys and about one-quarter African American. A boy asked a question and, as it was answered, Nicole raised her hand.

"Yes, Nicole?" queried the teacher. As he answered her question, he added another equation to the board.

"I did that part," said Nicole, "but. . . ."

He responded with a series of guiding questions, which she answered. "You just need to slow down and take your time. Don't be in a rush to plug in any old number," he encouraged her before taking the next question.

Turning to the day's assignment, the teacher demonstrated how to check the accuracy of answers and urged the students to do so. Nicole bent over her paper and began to fill her paper with neat, bold numbers. She pulled on a long curl of dark hair absently. The boy next to her drew a detailed hot rod.

"For homework, turn to pages 230 and 231, numbers 13 to 24," said the teacher. "Pick four problems and do them for tomorrow. Choose the ones that are hard for you so you can get help before the semester exam. Don't forget to see me before or after school if you need more help."

The bell rang. Nicole put on her jacket, dug in her purse for a brush and pulled it through her hair. Stacking her books, she seemed not to hear the teacher's final words about tomorrow's test.

"I just got my hair cut and I hate it," she said in a disgusted voice. Peering at the notes I took while observing the class, she wrinkled her nose and asked with a half grin, "What bad things did you write about me?"

"I just wrote what I saw in class," I replied. "What makes you think I wrote something bad?"

"I'm always doing something bad," she said with a shrug.

"Don't worry. Everybody's nervous when they see somebody taking notes about them," I said. "I just have to write it down so I don't forget the details."

"Oh, OK," she said, brightening up. Then she whispered conspiratorially, "Isn't he gorgeous?" She nodded toward a slight boy with wavy hair and the beginnings of a mustache.

> When I can get her to work and to think about things, she doesn't do that bad. She sometimes feels she is working hard, but I ask for homework and it's at home. I plan to give her an incomplete. I'll base her first quarter grade on the second quarter. I mean, I understand a little about the home problems and all that.
>
> She has a tendency to get frustrated because she thinks she understands it, and then it doesn't work out the way she thought. She has trouble remembering how to solve the equations; we learned that earlier in the year when she was absent so much. The first part of the quarter, she was coming to see me during her study hall for help, but I'm not real sure it wasn't to get out of study hall. She may have wanted some attention, too.
>
> She really doesn't strike me as rebellious. The kids tolerate her to a certain extent. It's not like she's an outcast or that she causes all the problems.
>
> — Nicole's algebra teacher

Study Hall, 9:55 a.m.

As Nicole took her assigned seat, Aileen stuffed a note into her hand. "This'll be a good one!" Nicole said with anticipation.

> Big Sis,
>   Yes, he's kissed me and he is a real gentleman.
> I can't tell you or anybody else, not even him how

much i like him. Every time i think about him i get all crazy inside, like i'm on a fun ride. Do you think if someone else told him how much i care or fell for him, do you think he would understand?

Well, gotta go, have to get some ZZZZ's.

Little Sis

Nicole shared this note with me and then rummaged through her papers for another:

Nicole,

Hey Chick what's up. Not much here. that's cool about the $120.00 you got from Greg. if you see Keith tell him to tell Tom G. that I want to meet him. God he's so fine. Well thanks

F/F Julie

P.S. find out if Tom has a girlfriend. O.K.?

Nicole explained, "See, I was going out with this guy and . . . you know. . . . Well, then he told me he got VD from me. So, I said I didn't think so, but my mom takes me to the doctor — it was humiliating! And I was fine! So my mom says to tell him I was pregnant. So, I did and he said to find out how much an abortion costs. Well, I didn't really call but I told him $250, but I only expected him to pay half. So two weeks later, he gives me $120!" She grinned, as if surprised but satisfied that the boy, an Asian-American, got what he deserved.

About 70 students filled half the chairs in the double room. Walking down the aisle, Aileen stopped to chat with Nicole and slipped her another note. An African American boy also walked by, stopped to touch the beer patch over the front pocket of Nicole's shirt; they smiled and chatted before he moved on. "He used to tease me when I ran track," she explained. "He said I ran like a bird. I run straight up but I was fast."

"You run track?" I asked.

"I used to. I used to be in basketball, too," she shrugged. "But not no more. Grades."

Finally, Nicole took out a calculator and her math book and wiggled into a comfortable position. A few minutes later, she was at the teacher's desk. She moved around the room, exchanged words with another boy, and returned to her desk, the boy watching her progress. She propped a foot on the chair in front of her as its occupant complained mildly.

"Check *you* out!" she retorted in a friendly skirmish. The foot remained.

Before the period was over, Nicole conferred, math book in hand, with three more boys; accepted another note from Aileen and melodramatically advised her to write on her face, "Oh, baby, I l-o-v-e you;" offered to "beat up" a boy who was kicking Aileen's desk (she told me that she was "everybody's bodyguard"); and offered to bring me notes from home "that I don't even let my mom read." At the sound of the bell she left. The boy who touched her shirt walked out with her; his hand firmly placed on her shoulder.

> Even after I've gotten short with her, Nicole will turn around and say, "nice day." She's cooperative but she will talk until I tell her not to. I had her up for detention one day and she talked non-stop. She had come in with a forged pass. When I called her on it, she was up-front and that was when she served detention.
>
> I find her moody. When she's feeling good, she's real social and talks a lot. When she's angry, she's quiet, sometimes puts her head down on her desk, mutters under her breath.
>
> Sometimes, she'll come back to my desk and start talking and, sometimes, I'll let her stay there. I don't want to make more of it than it is but I really get the sense that she needs somebody just to listen to her. I get the impression that she's got a lot of problems with her home life — that's what she was talking about with me when she was up for detention.
>
> — study hall teacher

Physical Education, 10:50 a.m.

The first of two volleyball games began. Nicole overpowered her serves, then giggled or stamped her foot. She volleyed energetically, good at both the net and the baseline. She laughed when she fell, robot-danced when she scored a point, congratulated teammates with a high-five slap of the hands, and participated in any jokes in her area of the court. She separated two squabbling boys and showed them where to stand. Her frequent laugh was a distinctive rat-a-tat-tat followed by a shrill screech, sometimes delivered arms akimbo, back arched.

As one ball crossed the net toward her team, Nicole called "Out!" before it touched the ground.

"You can't call it out before it touches the ground!" yelled an opponent.

"It was out! Didn't you see it?" she countered, throwing out her arms.

"It hadn't even touched the ground yet!" argued another opponent.

"You could see it was gonna go out!" Nicole said, giving the player a don't-jive-me look.

Both sides appealed to the teacher who didn't raise her eyes from the paper she was writing on as she said, "It has to touch the ground."

Nicole's mouth hung open for a moment in surprise and disgust. "When were the rules changed?"

She returned to play without resentment, however, and agreed when someone said, "We're having fun!"

Lunch, 11:45 a.m.

Nicole and I shared lunch four times, twice in the school cafeteria and twice at fast-food restaurants. Regardless of the cold, she always smoked a cigarette with a regular group of friends just off school grounds. Once, as we finished lunch at Burger Haven, Gloria drove up, flopped down next to Nicole, and complained about parenthood and marriage. Accepting Gloria's offer of a one-block ride back to school, Nicole was tempted when Gloria asked, "Sure you don't want to come on with me?"

"God, that woulda been fun to skip this afternoon — especially since we have *Julius Caesar* in English today. I hate *Julius Caesar*! Before, I woulda done it." She sighed, then in a determined voice concluded, "But not now. I've been absent too much and I wanna graduate."

General Business, 1:15 p.m.

The teacher asked the class to take out the typed notes she had given them. Some asked for another copy, and she had a few on hand to share. Aileen asked for a belt and flashed her belly-button in the first of many attention-seeking behaviors. Nicole and the teacher shared a brief private conversation, as two girls privately discussed their relationships with older men. "He had to get married, but then she had a miscarriage," one said. "They've only been married for six months and they're already planning to get a divorce."

5

The teacher guided an oral review of different kinds of check endorsements, money orders, telegraphic money orders, travelers' checks, bank drafts. Nicole raised her hand and was called on a couple of times. Once, she blurted out an answer to another student's question. The teacher didn't object but extended the answer with additional information. Nicole french-braided her hair, made a face to show me she was bored, rested her head on her desk, chuckled when Aileen ostentatiously answered a question, and then pointed to herself, clowning to others that she, not Aileen, had known the correct answer.

Someone entered the room and gave Nicole a slip of paper. She left immediately for the office of her counselor.

"Your stepdad just called," the counselor told her. "He got a note from your PE teacher saying that you haven't dressed six times in PE and that your grade is going to be dropped four letters."

"I forget to bring my clothes sometimes, but I didn't think it was that much," she responded anxiously. "I borrowed clothes a few times."

"Did you know about this?" the counselor asked.

"No, but it's my fault," she responded. "Boy, am I going to be restricted."

"What about your court date? How's that going?"

She told him the date and that she thought she would be sentenced to time in the county Youth Detention Center. "I'm paying for my own lawyer."

"Are your parents anxious or angry?"

"No," Nicole responded vaguely. "My mom isn't crazy about having to take off from work to go to court but that's all. I haven't seen my stepdad much lately 'cause he's working evenings."

"How about you? How are you taking it?"

"Oh, I'm fine. I won't get worried until I get there," she said, looking unperturbed.

"Well, try to do as well as you can before the semester ends. Your attendance has really improved and I think your grades are up, too." He gave her a pass. "Do you think you can get your mind on biology? Do you need a few minutes?"

"Nah, I'm fine," Nicole said as she retrieved her books from the room and headed for biology. "I don't think they should take you out of class like that," she muttered, "unless it's really important. You're not learning. And he's always, like, prying into my personal life. I think he should just ask about my grades."

It's hard to pinpoint Nicole. There are some days when she is on target and does well in class. There are other days when it's as if she's somewhere else. All she cares about is who Aileen went to lunch with.

She had a real attendance problem first semester. They have a new attendance policy that, if you miss more than nine days, you don't get credit for the semester. Apparently, they gave her a break and let her make up the work she missed. She seemed to buckle down. I don't know — maybe she realized that we were helping her. I spent quite a bit of time writing out all her missing assignments. She had a month to get it done, but the deadline came and went. I spent time waiting on her to take a test and she didn't show.

She doesn't turn in half her homework and then gets an A + on the test. Academically, she definitely has the potential to do well. She does seem to care about how she does and she's proud when she makes a good grade, but I don't think she's quite motivated. In class, she does fine.

I used to have her in the back of the room and she was easily distracted. Now, she sits right in front of me, and I think that gives us a little better rapport. When she sat at the back with her friends, I think she just saw me as the teacher. Now, maybe I'm a person, too.

— general business teacher

Biology, 2:10 p.m.

Nicole distributed plastic bags containing earthworms for dissection.

There was much talk and laughter. As usual, Nicole contributed to the noise.

The teacher raised his voice, "OK, let's get started." His expression was serious. He projected a transparency of a dissected earthworm, identifying seminal vesicles and seminal receptacles, which the students had to find on their specimens. Then they had to label the parts on mimeographed drawings.

"During mating," he explained, "two worms line up head-to-tail so that the seminal vesicles of one attach to the seminal receptacles of the other." The explanation elicited no giggles. "On tomorrow's test," he continued, "there will be pinned worms with parts for you to identify. I can guarantee one of those parts will be a seminal vesicle. If anyone can't find these parts, put your hand up and I'll help you."

Nicole, among others, raised her hand. She and her lab partner, Samantha, were talking and laughing at their table in a back corner of the room. A girl passed by and fluffed Nicole's hair. The teacher arrived at their table and directed them to open up their worm more. He indicated the correct organs, then moved on.

The teacher resumed the lecture, but the students' attention was scattered. Eventually, the students returned their materials. Some students misplaced pins or scissors and others put the implements where they belonged. The teacher stacked the dissection pans.

The school day ended with the sound of the bell and his final reminder to study for tomorrow's test.

> *Nicole craves attention. She's been carrying an ice bag around on her finger for two days. I think she's using it to gain my attention and, secondly, to go to the nurse. She can be gone ten or fifteen minutes.*
>
> *She's already missed darned close to twenty days in my class. She's been truant. This is not a question of the girl being sick. I get a feeling that she feels — maybe rightfully so, I don't know — her parents may be too tough on her, too strict. That may be totally incorrect, I don't know. But, since she came back, she hasn't done very much, and she is not an unintelligent girl. There are brief periods in which she seems to be very interested, in which she asks questions.*
>
> *Sometimes she is sullen when I correct her. Earlier in the year, there were times she just came in and put her head down. Don't get me wrong — she's not at all unfriendly. For the most part, she's a polite girl. She will interact with certain members of the class, but there are some who do not think very highly of her.*
>
> — *biology teacher*

After School

Nicole babysat about three hours after school each day and about five hours on weekends. She arrived at her babysitting job and entered without knocking. Taking off her shoes at the door, she called, "Hi."

Tony was eight. He was watching cartoons on television and playing with Attack Ants, a contemporary version of tin soldiers. Nicole sat by him on the carpet and asked him about his ants. The two played quietly, changed the TV channel, and glanced at the set occasionally. When "The Brady Bunch" appeared on the screen, they were more attentive and attacked each other's ants only intermittently. Nicole distracted Tony to win a battle and he yelled, "You cheated! I'm gonna show your butt up!"

They looked through groceries in sacks on the kitchen counter. Nicole got a diet soft drink. Tony pulled apple juice frozen on a fork from the freezer.

"I got in a fight with the fastest guy in school," he told her mournfully. "He called me a F-A-G, and we started kicking each other."

"Did he get in trouble?" Nicole asked sympathetically.

"No!" Tony exploded. "He lied his guts out!"

A moment later he asked, "See my new glasses? See how they bend?"

"They must have been expensive," she flattered him.

"A hundred and eighty dollars. We got them at Lensmakers last night."

"Are you supposed to be wearing them?"

"I don't have to," he said. "Oh, crap! Look what just fell on my lap — my apple juice!"

"Did any get on the floor?"

"No," he answered, as the frozen remains fell on the carpet.

"You better throw that away. It's dirty now," said Nicole.

Tony shook his head.

"Please?"

He began to suck the frozen juice again. "Oh, boy! 'Gilligan's Island!' "

Later, he went outside to play basketball. Tony's mother arrived and smilingly told me that Nicole was their favorite babysitter.

Nicole at Home

Nicole lived with her mother and stepfather in an attractively decorated mobile home in a tidy trailer park. Five Siamese cats, which her mother bred and sold, met her at the door. Nicole glanced inside a pizza box — "Yuk!" — and shoved it in the microwave.

Using a spray cleaner, Nicole wiped glass tabletops, door, and storm door while listening to rap music. "See," she said, "this was full at the start of the week." It's only about a third full now. My mother is a clean freak. I do this every day." She polished the furniture, transferred clothes from washer to dryer, and fed the fish. She examined the glass chimneys of hurricane lamps. "Disgusting!" she said as she washed off microscopic dust.

A car horn sounded and she stepped outside for a few minutes. "Roger," she explained. "He's a sweetheart."

Changing the tape mid-song from rock to country, she swallowed a birth control pill and explained that her periods were too frequent and cramps were painful.

She had forgotten to get cigarettes, so we went out for some.

Returning, she made me a thick ham sandwich for supper and said she was worried that I might be bored. We watched "The Cosby Show," which she said she loved. She lip-synched part of the dialogue. She cleaned the cat box during a commercial.

I was surprised to find this girl, described as headstrong and boy crazy, spending the entire evening cleaning house. "Does your mother appreciate this work?" I asked.

"Sometimes. I mean, I'm sure she does, but she doesn't always say so."

Her mother called and Nicole catalogued the chores she had completed.

She came to my attention after nine days of absence. She was at the point of not getting credit in any course. I'm very hesitant to withdraw credit. We tried all the avenues rather than being hard right to start with. We had a conference with her parents in October. Nicole accepted responsibility. She said all the right words and was very plausible, which made me suspicious. It creates some doubt when somebody has that little speech all ready to go. You see a lot of that, particularly in the brighter students — and I think this one is fairly bright. But the meeting had an effect, and it shows on her attendance record. I think maybe the moving around that she did from school to school — I think three moves last year, her freshman year — hurt her.

In December, her stepdad called for about the tenth time in two or three days to say that he was coming to take her to Round House, a time-out and runaway shelter. She had stolen the family car, and they had just found out about it. That same month, we asked her why she had been absent several times for a particular class. She said, "I was going behind Hamburger Haven to sell drugs to pay for gas when I took the car at night." I said, "What?" because this is not your common everyday admission. She'd gone over with another girl, a dropout, to sell marijuana at noontime. That's how they were financing their escapades. We talked to her about the consequences for that kind of thing, but I don't know if she took it seriously. She said they'd stopped.

I'm becoming cynical, the longer I stay at this desk, about the role of parents. I see a lot of kids really screwed up, and you don't get that screwed up that young without somebody helping you. I don't know all of Nicole's background. I know that she has a stepfather, who, at times, seems genuinely caring and, at times, antagonistic. In his estimation, Nicole got away with a lot of things and somebody needed to clamp down on her. I get mixed feelings from him and the mother. Some of the things that they were wanting us to do were clearly not our function. I'm not into chastising and punishing children for behaviors at home.

She's very mature — physically and probably sexually. I don't know that Nicole's promiscuous, but promiscuity is common for kids that don't have guidance from home. Why? A product of moving around; a product of parents too busy. And children of alcoholics quite often feel responsible for their parents' alcoholism. You can't say parents don't care — they just don't know how to care.

— director of student services

We started talking on a regular basis in October as a result of an attendance conference with her parents. Nicole would talk about her home life — her mother considering divorce or separation from her current husband and getting involved with a former boyfriend, other people coming to the house to go out drinking with or without the husband. Her parents work at a liquor store, so they come home with alcohol, especially her stepdad. She described him as an alcoholic. Blowups were frequent with her stepfather, less frequent with her mother. Nicole would say it was her fault. We worked on helping her realize when these incidents were occurring and how to cope with them — some strategies. That seemed to work.

One of the moves last year, her freshman year, was to live with her real father. She had major troubles with him, but she didn't get into those with me. I do know that, at night when she would take the car, drugs were involved.

I think her home life puts her at risk. Her attitude, knowing something is wrong but going ahead with it, puts her at risk. Plus the alcoholic environment at the house and the on-again-off-again relationship between her mother and stepfather.

She knows the importance of staying in school because she had the opportunity to be out of here months ago when she turned 16. If you're not in school, it's hard to keep up, hard to make up all the work once you turn things around — which she did. It was a lot of work to stay and catch up, but she did. If she can get through another year, she will have enough credits to graduate with her class. For some reason, I think she's going to stay with us — hope so because, with all of the trouble that she has, she's really a likable student.

— counselor

This fall she was skipping school, and we were trying to work with her. She had obvious family problems. At one time, I think, she was living with a boyfriend. [For about two months early in the 1988-89 academic year, Nicole shared an apartment with two friends, Jenny and Matt.] She was in my office from time to time, but most of these episodes were related to what was going on at home. She does these off-the-wall stunts — taking the car — bold things for someone her age.

She always appeared to be listening. Occasionally, we would hear that she'd done some dumb things, but when I saw her, she always appeared to be receptive. It's been my experience that, down the road a couple of years some of what everybody has been telling a kid soaks in and they begin to do OK. Some parents don't care; some give up. Those who keep trying, even if the kid is misbehaving — those kids have a lot better chance.

— associate principal

I've given up on her. I'm going to exist until she gets married or goes to college and that's it. Last fall, I questioned whether she would even finish school. I don't know what changed — in seventh and eighth grades, she was an A and B student. I just don't understand her. I never know what to expect. I don't know whether I'm too strict on her and she feels like breaking loose, or whether it's "Who cares? I'm going to do what I want to do."

I don't think Nicole is much of a drinker; she does it to be with her friends and not that often. Once she told me she had drank two Budweisers. I didn't smell any beer on her breath, and, owning a liquor store, I should know. If she had, she ought to give up drinking because she was really out of it. I'm not sure about marijuana and drugs. I have no idea what she was doing.

She has a bad problem with lying. It's just to protect herself; just when she gets caught in a situation, she lies. She denies smoking.

Last year, she went to live with my sister upstate. When she left, I felt relieved. I wasn't worried about her. My sister is probably stricter than I am. But her aunt wouldn't tolerate the lying, so she sent her home. I thought, "Yeah, I knew the vacation would end soon." Later that year, she went to live with her father. I had some reservations about that. I got two different stories. Her father said she was sneaking out at night, and she said that he was — I can't say making sexual advances — but making her feel uncomfortable.

The car has been a serious problem. The first time she took it was about a year ago. She was just turning fifteen. I had taken the car for new tires and noticed a big dent. Then,

I found a note in Nicole's room saying she'd taken the car and backed it into a garage. I was ready to strangle her. I was afraid my insurance wasn't going to cover it.

I suspected she was taking the car. There would be either more gas or less gas than before or I'd find it in a different gear. She would deny it. I decided I needed help last year when there was a military air base sticker on it. That's federal, and she wasn't insured or licensed. So, I went to the police station. They talked to her, but it didn't do a whole lot of good.

When school started this year, all hell broke loose. She decided she'd rather move out than go by my rules. One day, she came down to the liquor store driving a car. I guess I wanted her back home, but I couldn't physically force her, so I called and reported that she was driving this car. She got a ticket, but she continued to stay in this apartment with these two friends until they decided they didn't want her there and moved her back home.

Then, I suspected that she was taking the car again. I never understood what she was doing in this town at one or two in the morning. One night, I heard her on the phone, heard the front door close, heard the car start, and I called the police. She got her second ticket.

She's going to court for it tomorrow. I'm not really worried because I've talked to her attorney, and I know what's going to happen. She's going to be put on probation for a year. She'll have to report to somebody, and they'll give her guidelines to go by. This sounds terrible, but I'm looking forward to it because she is going to be responsible to somebody else for a while. The probation officer tried to scare her by saying she might spend some time in the Youth Detention Center. Actually, it might be good if somebody with some authority put a jolt to her because she's going to be in big trouble if she continues through life like this.

The school has been very cooperative. I feel Nicole could get more help if she would ask, but she's there to socialize. I don't think there's too much chance of her deciding to go to college; I have hopes, but I really doubt it. They're keeping an eye on her for me this year because of the skipping she did. If I have a problem, I can telephone the assistant principal. I've talked a lot with a counselor, but I almost feel like he's given up on her, too.

We've had a counselor from Round House meet with the family since, maybe, October. He was looking for something medical because he couldn't understand why she does what she does, but there was nothing there.

She has a lot of good qualities if she would use them, but she doesn't. I've tried everything: rewarding her, taking the phone or stereo or TV away, but she watches anyway when I'm gone. I can't even get her to quit smoking — here I sit smoking. I'd just be wasting my breath if I told her about drugs. I guess I've kind of used her stepfather because she can put a lot of pressure on me — she won't speak to me or she'll give me a rough time. She won't give him a rough time. Her brother Jim is in Texas in the service. Bob is here in town, but any guidance he tries to give her, she resents.

Nicole is my youngest, and she was the only girl. I wanted a girl real bad. She never seemed to take advantage of it when she was younger and I always thought I could depend on her. She'd come home on time; she was good in school. We would play school and she caught on real quick. I don't know what happened. She was only about six at the time of the divorce. I think it bothered her, but she seemed to adjust fairly well. I think we had a close relationship until she was about twelve.

We're trying to cut down on help at the liquor store, so I work evenings. Nicole gets home from babysitting about five and I get home about 10, so we don't spend a lot of time together. On the weekends, she'd rather do things with her friends. I think any more time and we'd probably be ready to strangle each other.

— Nicole's mother

I guess my friends would say I'm wild, crazy, and understanding. I'm a clown. I'll say stupid things and everybody will laugh. I like attention; I'll admit it. Some of my friends are good students, but some are not. I usually study by myself because if I'm with a friend, there ain't no way it's going to get done. Well, with Samantha, we get it done. We listen to music and we laugh and it gets done. But, with Aileen, we'd start talking about a guy — who her boyfriend is this week or who it will be next weekend, same thing with me, though.

It's kind of weird, you know. I can talk to some of the teachers just like teenagers. Like the study hall teacher, she was real fun to talk to. But, some of the teachers are so uppity and trying to dress in a little tie and be all perfect. I've talked with the assistant principal a couple of times when my mom and stepdad were in fights. She'd say, "Just stay out of it," but it won't work. I've heard that same thing over and over again.

When I went to that October attendance meeting, I said, "I realize I've got things I've got to do and I'm going to." I was lying out of my teeth. But, it worked; I got my credit, and I have been going to school. No skipping. Doing my homework. I guess, since I lied, I had to live up to it. I wanted to.

I did really good in elementary and junior high — honors, sports, everything. I was one of the popular people. Then

I started getting in arguments with my mother. She would say things to me I didn't like. So I moved from my mother's house, and I started going downhill. Everything's been in a two-month cycle. I think it's because I don't like the way they live or I just get bored. But you can't keep running away.

I started getting in trouble probably the summer after seventh grade. I hung out with people that were in high school. I looked older, but I wasn't being responsible like an older person. I start thinking about the past like, "God, that was stupid!" Your parents say, "When you're older, you're going to thank me for this." But, then, you don't care.

Second quarter of my freshman year, last year, I moved in with my aunt upstate. Then we got in a fight over my grades. So, fourth quarter, I went and lived with my dad. While I was there, my stepmom and the two kids packed up and moved. My father and I were left together about a month, and he tried something on me. I was standing up, and he had his arms around me and was rubbing me up and down. I called a friend to pick me up. I got my checks where I'd been working, called my mom, and bought a bus ticket back home. My mom told me to call the cops, and I did but they said they couldn't do anything because he didn't get in my clothes.

So, I came back home and lived with my mother for the summer. After a week of school this year, I moved to an apartment with my friends, Jenny and Mait. My grades had gone to Ds and Fs third quarter of my freshman year. This year, my sophomore year, first quarter, I didn't pass anything because I wasn't going to school; I was at the apartment. I like to sleep in. I started drinking and getting in trouble.

I had a job at Big Burger. My mom had told me to lie about my age. Then, as soon as I moved into the apartment, she told them I was underage. Of course, they fired me, but they told me I could come back when I turned sixteen because I was a good worker. That was important then because I was paying rent.

One night when I was having supper with my mom and stepfather, my roommates brought over all my stuff. They were kicking me out. I wanted to live at home, but my mom said I couldn't unless I straightened up. So, I promised I would start going to school.

My parents divorced when I was about seven. My father had been going out on my mom. I remember one time when I was four he shoved her against the wall. I thought my older brothers would help, but they just stood there. So, I grabbed one of them big black skillets and knocked him over. My mom cried and hugged me.

People at school keep telling me to stay out of fights at home, but it don't work. Mom will say, "Nicole, come here. I need your support." What am I supposed to do?

My parents want me to make good grades, but I don't think my mom's really interested in my career plans. I told her I wanted a typewriter because I'm taking a typing class right now. She goes, "I wouldn't mind buying you a typewriter if I knew you were going to college."

I said, "Well, I am going to college."

She goes, "I want you to prove it to me first, and then we'll see about a typewriter."

My mom's always got work on her mind. She comes home in a bad mood, and she puts me in a bad mood. Then, I get mean towards her and that's not the way it should be. I wish they weren't so stressed.

We don't talk much, but when we do talk, she's real open about sex and drugs. That's one good thing. But she's a clean freak. Every morning I have to have my room spotless. Tonight, I've got to vacuum, fold the laundry, do the dishes. If I don't, I'm dead meat. I wait until fifteen minutes before she gets off to fold the clothes. I don't like to do them, but I like to have clean clothes.

It's when I'm depressed that I take the car or do something stupid. It's like I don't care if I get caught. When I'm on restriction, that's when the craving comes so bad. I've been on restriction a lot this year but it's my own fault. I've been a pain in the butt. Like, about the ticket for driving without a license. I don't blame my mom for reporting me. She's just doing what a parent tries to do to save her butt and mine.

I wasn't nervous when I walked in the courtroom. Then, the judge started going off on me and I thought, "You dickhead! Don't talk to me like that!" He said all my friends are hoodlums and I was a troublemaker and I was going to end up in jail. My attorney said I had improved at home. The state's attorney requested I get probation. The judge read the reports and decided without asking me. Then, he started talking about a weekend in the youth detention center.

I asked my attorney, "When am I going to be going?"

He goes, "Now."

Somebody came up and grabbed my arm and put handcuffs on me and hauled me out of the room. I didn't even get to say goodbye to my mom. They put me in this room and walked out. Then, we got in this van with bars and a screen thing and it took us to the detention center. We had to fill out all kinds of paperwork. They strip-searched me and made me take a shower and put on these clothes and go to my room. The strip-search took maybe 10 seconds. I was embarrassed but not to the point where I cried.

16

I had a bad cold. I bet I slept 16 to 18 hours a day. My mom bought me cherry cold medicine and nice cough drops. She took care of me.

I had four days — 78 hours — in the detention center, $141.06 in court costs, 40 hours of public service. I got a sheet of house rules like no smoking, do your chores, a curfew. I was to check in with my probation officer at police headquarters every Wednesday, but, when I met him, he told me I could come every other Wednesday.

I had 10 ways to kill that judge. I was outraged that he sent me to the detention center for something as little as driving without a license. I mean, it is an offense but it's not like getting caught with pot. Those kids get a $63 fine, a slap on the hand. I can't say it's unfair. He was trying to teach me a lesson. In the long run, it was best because I'm not going to get in trouble and go back there again. I realized how much I take for granted. The first thing I did when I got home was go in the bathroom all by myself, no one watching.

After I got back to school, the vice-principal called me in his office. I thought I was in trouble. He told me he wished they had contacted the school because he would have told them it was a bad idea. He was impressed by how much I've improved. I was surprised because he's like an ogre.

I'd like to go to [a state college]. I might be able to get in if I get my butt in gear, but I don't know. My grades are OK but I could do better. Just so much has happened in the past few years. I lost interest in everything. I want to get my graduation requirements taken care of. If you don't graduate, you ain't got nothing. My mother got her GED. She worked in a factory for eight years. I don't want to work in a factory. You need your diploma but, anymore, you need to go to college to get a job that pays good and that you'll like. I want to go to college and join the Marines; I've been planning that for about two years.

I thought about dropping out when I was living in the apartment. Everybody that I know that has dropped out says, "I'm glad I dropped out." Then, a couple of months later, "God, I wish I hadn't dropped out." You hear what they say; it sinks into your brain after you hear it so many times.

I've smoked pot maybe ten times. I've done speed once. I've never done cocaine or shot up or anything like that. I haven't smoked pot in probably six months. I don't need that stuff to have a good time. Some of those kids are screwing their lives up.

Once I had been drinking and I was stoned. We were in a truck and there was a girl driving. She wrecked it, but luckily nobody got hurt bad. It was a miracle. I think there's only been once or twice my friends have come over and drank but I wouldn't let them drive if they were totally wasted.

The guys act like sixth-graders. It's like one thing on their minds — bang. I tell them to back off and if they don't I use the old knee. Everybody knows how I am. I don't have the reputation of being an easy lay. My first boyfriend was a freshman and I was a sixth-grader. He'd come over when my mom wasn't home. I'd kiss him and hold hands. Then he started wanting to do other things and I was like, "I don't think so." Well, I ended up giving in completely. It was the summer I was twelve. I felt so terrible. My mom came home from work that day and I was crying. I couldn't tell her so I made up a lie. I finally told her two years later. She was real understanding because she got pregnant when she was in sixth grade. She told me, "Your body is yours. Don't let anybody do something with it that you don't want them to."

I wish I could quit smoking. I just wish I had more willpower. I want to care more about what I do — have more respect for myself, more morals. I decided I better get my butt in gear or I'd have to spend another year in school. Now, I've got my priorities straight. I ain't been in trouble. I don't lie anymore at all. I don't drink either. If I want to have fun, I go bowl or play pool. I have two jobs now — babysitting [about 20 hours a week] and I help out at my mom's liquor store.

I used to have an attitude of "Fuck it — if it gets done it gets done. If it don't, it don't. No sweat off my back." But it is. If I pass, I get the credit. I get to graduate. It's not what someone else does. If I want to get anything, I've got to earn respect. I've got to start doing what's expected of me and what I know is right.

Mom and I are becoming actual friends. She's a lot more supportive. I think she wants to help me. I want to have a good relationship with my mom. We sat down — my mom, my stepfather, and me. We talked about how we wanted to be as a family. My stepfather is drinking less. He's working now. There's no fighting.

I can honestly say that the change started when I started talking to you. I've had counselors, but they're dipwits. It was like you really cared. And I didn't really have anybody who cared. I guess at the start you didn't bitch at me. You were here and you listened and you were just so supportive.

— Nicole

The Case Study: Background and Methodological Notes

Phi Delta Kappa wanted to know about students considered to be at risk of school failure. Of all the stories, whose might be neglected? Perhaps the story of a white, middle-class girl —

attending school, living at home, in a small town's average-sized high school of 1,500 students, in a community of about 18,000 — would be neglected. Teachers and counselors at the school immediately agreed on a candidate: disarmingly candid Nicole.

Between December 1988 and March 1989, I spent about a dozen days on site: in classes, conferences, interviews; with school records; in the cafeteria; at the local burger joints, Nicole's house, and at the house where she babysits. I planned to blend in unobtrusively, but Nicole would have none of that. She seemed to relish having her footsteps dogged by a curious stranger. She stopped worrying about my note taking, acquiesced to my tape recorder, tried not to smile into the video camera when it, too, turned a relentless eye upon her. What would I like to know? Would I like to read this note from Aileen? What did I think she should do about her boyfriend? Did I agree this class was boring? Did I think that guy was cute?

She made research easy, but my role as researcher difficult. She undermined my attempts to recede into the background, insisted on seeing me as a person rather than as an observer, and invited me into her life.

Reflections

The adults in Nicole's life held contrasting opinions about Nicole's behavior and influences on it, and about her goals. The judge predicted and prescribed incarceration. Trying to be patient and flexible, teachers reacted to her attention-seeking and wondered about her home life. The assistant principal thought Nicole might find success within social standards if her parents could persevere during her apparent failure. The director of student services was less optimistic, largely blaming her parents for Nicole's being "screwed up," even as he acknowledged that they would care better for her if they knew how. Nicole's counselor — who, of the school personnel, interacted with her most — noted she'd survived considerable adversity, thought she'd stay to graduate if she could hang on a bit longer, and encouraged her to attend college. Most of the school people suspected that she was more promiscuous and involved with drugs than she evidenced in interviews and observations. Nicole's mother was not uncaring, but felt her emotional resources exhausted and her authority diminished. She could summon little consistence or flexibility. She believed both she and the school had done all they could. She attributed Nicole's missteps entirely to Nicole and wondered what happened to the well-behaved little girl who made good grades. Her stepfather did not meet me.

During the three months of the study, Nicole's attitude changed noticeably from it's-my-life defiance to it's-my-life-and-I-don't-want-to-blow-it responsibility. Throughout, she saw the negative consequences for her behavior as just. She saw that her effort was inconsistent but improving through her own conscious attempts. She expressed more and higher goals than any of the adults in her life perceived. I thought they would be surprised and heartened by her attentiveness to domestic chores, her work ethic outside school assignments, her fondness for children, her realistic attitude.

First and foremost, the disruptions in her family and living situation clearly undermined her academic motivation. Shifting family loyalties and frequent moves created instability and, probably, the attitude that life is essentially unstable. Second, her rebelliousness fueled family instability and contributed to a dysfunctional loop. Perhaps her rebelliousness would have remained within the bounds of typical teenage independence seeking if not for this vicious circle. Third, one manifestation of her rebelliousness was disregard for authority. Her willingness to escape rather than follow rules, to break the law, caused serious repercussions and grave concern.

Perhaps Nicole would have benefitted from more consistent, positive encouragement. But many cared about her, listened to her, encouraged her; sometimes they threatened or punished her. Remarkably, she credited them with acting in her best interests whether she liked their actions or not. Her sense of responsibility was puzzling. Why did she misbehave when she knew it would bring trouble? Why did she accept all the blame for situations she only partly controlled? I wondered, and she and her counselors wondered with me, without much explanation. Was her sense of responsibility, or overresponsibility, innate? Did she acquire it in the discontinuities of her life or by default from her parents?

Teachers and counselors were struck by her attention seeking, taken aback by her unsolicited frankness, skeptical that she wanted the kind of help she requested. They doubted she knew what constituted socially acceptable behavior. They bent rules for her, wondered what else to do, worried about what would become of her. Nicole expressed disdain for the faculty in general but genuine liking for teachers individually. The general business teacher seemed to have understood best that there was a difference between being seen as a teacher and as a person. Nicole branded as "dipwits" the counselors who had listened and advised, although she had sometimes initiated contact. Why had she felt differently about me? You listened, she said; others listened, I said. You cared, she said; others cared, I said. You advised me even when you weren't supposed to, she said; I thought I hadn't, but what I said was that others had advised her. Again, the difference seemed to be a matter of personalization. Not without irony, I found that I, who was to have personalized her in my case study, had been personalized by her.

Primarily, the attention she sought seemed a plea for someone to listen and understand without criticizing or directing. She needed to know that her concerns were taken seriously. She needed to know that someone had confidence in her. She needed to know that someone cared about her.

━━━━━

The summer after I had finished writing my case study of Nicole, I brought a copy of the final report to her school along with a copy of the accompanying videotape. Three of her teachers watched those portions of the tape that showed classroom scenes and faculty-staff interviews; they were not shown Nicole's interview segments. They were given similar sections of the final report. The biology teacher told me that late in the spring semester he had intercepted a note from Nicole to a classmate in which she indicated concern that she might be pregnant. During final examinations, although her grades in biology were passing, Nicole stood off-campus smoking, and so she failed. This seems to have occurred with all her classes. I wondered if perhaps she thought she was pregnant and that her life would soon change dramatically; perhaps she saw no point in taking final exams.

Later the same day, I brought two copies of the final report to Nicole's home along with a copy of the videotape. One copy was for Nicole's mother (interviews with Nicole and the faculty and staff had been excised). The other copy was for Nicole (interviews with her mother and the faculty and staff had been excised). When I arrived, Nicole explained that she and her mother were at odds because her stepfather had been put in jail for burglary; Nicole had refused her mother's request to perjure herself in testifying in his defense. It was necessary for us to go to her high school to view the videotape.

Driving to the school, Nicole said, "I have a million things to tell you!" She told me that she had been romantically involved with a 30-year-old man earlier in the summer. When she suspected he was married, she told her mother, who invited the man and his wife to come for discussion. I could hardly imagine this foursome's conversation. Nicole did not mention how the school year had ended.

When we arrived at the school, I showed Nicole the classroom segments of the videotape and her own interviews. She had cut her hair over the summer and, seeing how photogenic she had been with her long, dark curls, she remarked, "God, maybe I shouldn't have got my hair cut off." She grew quiet, watching intently as she heard herself talk about her improvement at school — raising grades, increasing respect, even taking home papers to grade for one of her teachers. She heard herself talk about her improving relationship with her mother, going to church, college plans, spending her money more wisely, not lying, her realization that it was up to her to make the most of her life and her intention to do so.

I had expected to talk with Nicole about the end of the school year and her plans; the "million things" she had wanted to say. But after watching herself on tape, she was silent. I later wondered if she had been sobered by the realization of how well she had been doing, how much she had thrown away.

22

After a few futile attempts at an informal interview, I asked her whether she would like our relationship to continue and, if so, in what form. I was profoundly startled at her half-joking reply: "Let me live with you." My mind raced. It seemed highly unlikely that her mother would approve. The youngest of my three children, a son still living at home, was a month older than Nicole and very unlike her. My husband and I were at odds and, although I didn't know it at the time, would separate within six months. Thinking I had little stability to offer her, I responded to the joking sound in her tone. We decided that since we lived in different but nearby communities we would talk on the phone and get together from time to time. She asked for a copy of the parts of the tape she had seen.

Early in the fall when the tape she'd requested was finished, I called before bringing it to her. Nicole's mother said she had moved to Oklahoma to live with an aunt. I was unable to get a telephone number or address. I sent the tape to her mother and called the school. Nicole had not requested her records, which suggested that she had dropped out of school. I checked with the counselors several times over the next few months but the situation remained unchanged.

She telephoned me in the spring. We arranged to get together for breakfast but unknowingly selected a restaurant that didn't open until lunch time. I waited in the parking lot, tried her home, and went to the business where she'd said she was working. Her coworkers didn't know where she was. I went to her mother's place of business and got an address where Nicole and a boyfriend were living. It was a long way out in the country, a rickety apartment over a defunct meat locker. No one was home. I left a note on the door that remains unanswered.

Months later, a Christmas card to Nicole's mother's home resulted in a phone call when Nicole came to visit. One of the things she said left a strong impression: "A lot of things have happened since you saw me last. You wouldn't know me now." We were unable to get together on that occasion. She said she expected to move back to town in February and would call me then. I called her mother in February; no Nicole.

There has been no further contact and little information to be gained in periodic requests. I called Nicole's mother again. The male who answered the phone said, "Nobody here gets along with Nicole." Her mother said Nicole was living in a small city in northern Illinois and gave me the phone number of an aunt. When I called, an uncle answered the phone. "She lived with us for a while," he said, "but now she's living in an apartment with a couple of girlfriends in a different town. They don't have a phone." Nor did he have any idea how I might reach Nicole. He said, "she stops by from time to time," and took my name and phone number to give her.

I hope she will call.

ROACH, CASE STUDY OF A MURDERER

Roach was not his real name but one he earned for his habit of collecting the roaches, or unsmoked ends, of marijuana cigarettes from older brothers and friends. He was the little kid, always hanging around the older ones, trying to keep up and make his way in a family that eventually included eight children. His dad, a truck driver, spent days on the road, often returning home in exhausted silence. His mother stayed at home making ends meet and trying to keep the family of ten together on a very limited income. It was the second marriage for both parents, and Roach was their second child.

You have to drive two hours from the city across the rolling hills to find the small town where Roach grew up. You could look across the fertile valley to the little town perched on the hills and find his house, nestled in a poorer section of town. Typically, the yard and house were full of kids — both those who lived there and those who came to play. Roach was there, playing with his friends. Some parts of his life he did not enjoy, and he avoided these in his own secret ways.

His mother told me about Roach, calling him by his real name. Lovingly she picked up his picture, and with tears in her eyes, described him. "I had a hard time when he was born. He like ta' died. And when he was a baby, it took him a long time to learn how to walk. He wasn't fast like the others. When he was two years old, he got a fever and was in a coma in the hospital. He had a real high fever. I hate to say it because he is my own kid, but do you think that could have done something to his brain?"

Medical care was a luxury and except for the free shots at the health department, the family could not afford doctor's fees. Only an emergency or serious illness warranted trips to the doctor or hospital. The question of whether Roach was mentally affected by his illness was never answered.

When Roach was fifteen years old, he was sentenced to death for killing a man. At the time of this interview, he had just been placed in the general population of a maximum security prison. This study is not about the murder, which captured the interest of the national media. Rather it is about the young man and some of his family, school, and community relationships, which may have influenced the outcome of his life.

After the murder, Roach's father left. When asked about his dad, Roach said that the main problem was that he was never around enough. Roach's parents divorced shortly after Roach was convicted. His mother left town, and like many family members of prisoners, moved to another town nearer the prison where her son sat on death row.

I interviewed Roach's mother and sister in their living room. In the background a Christmas tree, family pictures, and other treasures evoked an image of pleasant family life. I wondered how a disaster like this could happen in such a family. On the surface, they were the ideal nuclear family: two parents in the home, father employed, mother caring for the children, and some very bright brothers and sisters. The boys played baseball and other sports in the neighborhood vacant lot and on local teams. The parents did not drink and, while not well educated, were able to read. The older sisters read to the younger children and helped care for them. Work was valued, and family ties were close.

Roach Goes to School

Roach began having problems with school almost from the beginning. He said he received at least 10 spankings in kindergarten because he misbehaved. "I hated school. I always hated it," he said. When I asked him if he had been treated badly at school, he said, "No, I just hated it and didn't want to be there."

Some of Roach's characteristics were admirable. He didn't blame others for things he did. In spite of his hatred for school, he never blamed teachers or school authorities for his failures but simply expressed his steady preference to be away from school. Other family members confirmed Roach's school problems. "Some teachers seem to think you were bad or not very smart just because you were poor or because of who you were. They put you in a lower class and you could never get out until you left," said Roach's sister. She explained how moving to another school in another state had allowed her to be herself for the first time.

Roach's resistance to school became a consistent pattern of behavior. His mother said he had been locked in the classroom for misbehavior while the teacher took the other children out to recess. Roach climbed out a window and ran home, where his mother defended him against the school classroom aide who came to retrieve him. He seemed to be a special favorite of his mother perhaps because of his early illness.

Roach had trouble learning. "It was easy at first. They gave you As on everything when you were little, but it got harder in the third grade. Then in fourth grade, I figured out that I couldn't read. I hated it when they called on me to read out loud. It was embarrassing."

The school responded to Roach's problems by providing special reading classes. When that did not help, Roach was placed in special education in his junior high years. "That was too easy," Roach said. "You just sit around and do little papers that you can do in a minute, then you can just do nothing. They always passed you." School still was the place Roach wanted to get away from, and he often skipped classes. One day the special education teacher warned him that if he missed a certain number of days, he would be suspended. This was good news to Roach, who had been hoping for that very result. He missed the required number of days and got suspended.

Suspension became a habit. "You just hit somebody on Monday and get suspended for a week. That way you don't have to go to school and it's legal. They used to spank me but I figured out that teachers can't make you take a whipping like your folks. If you don't take your licks, they suspend you."

One might think that Roach was lazy, but that was not the case. Roach delivered newspapers and worked as a ticket taker for a trucking firm. He valued working and earning a salary and was a responsible worker who didn't miss the chance to be on the job, even in his early teens.

The Good Teacher

I asked Roach if he had ever had a teacher who really was able to help him. Yes, he said, he had had an English teacher who was very good. "She would always tell you the assignment, but then she stayed up in the front of the room and gave help. She didn't just sit at her desk and grade papers. I liked her because she helped everybody and didn't make you embarrassed if you didn't know something. I learned a lot in her class and got good grades. She was fair."

The Secret

Roach kept a terrible secret from all but a few of his friends — he began to sneak beer from his teenage brothers. With so many children in the family, no one paid particular attention or noticed that he had started drinking beer at age six. "I didn't really like the taste but I liked the way it made me feel." Roach's drinking became a regular pattern, and he got really drunk for the first time when he was eight years old.

Roach also started collecting the ends of marijuana cigarettes his brothers and older friends used. He couldn't get one all the time, but when he could get a roach, he smoked it. "You don't take it to school, just smoke it on the way to school. That way you don't get caught." By the time Roach was in the middle grades, he used alcohol and marijuana whenever he could get them. Eventually Roach used most of the available drugs of his day. The first time his mother knew he had been drinking was when he was about 10 or 11 years old — the police picked him up for riding his bicycle while intoxicated. His mother blamed the incident on his having helped a friend do cleaning at a bar. That's not the way Roach told it, however.

Neither the school nor his parents knew that Roach had become a consistent user of drugs and alcohol. It seemed improbable that his family had not been aware of his drug abuse, but Roach's brother did seem surprised when I shared this information with him for the first time. Roach told me about his drug abuse one day in his cell, explaining, "I don't want some other kid to wind up here like I did."

The Other Side of the Law

Looking at the handsome, personable young man before me, I had trouble seeing the other side of his life. He described his other occupation, his criminal job.

Roach began to shoplift at about age 10. He would steal candy bars and other merchandise to sell to buy drugs and other things. Sometimes he would get caught by the police, "but they don't do anything to a little kid," he said. "They just try to scare you, but I was wise to all that. I talked to my friends and they said that the law wouldn't do nothing to you. They just put you on probation. You have to see them once a week. You just tell them what they want to hear and they don't bother you. I did pretty good for a kid. I can't really go into all the details but I did a lot [robbery] and they never touched me until this time."

Roach described his relationship with the police. He had been successful in avoiding arrest even though he regularly stole things from homes. Prior to his arrest for murder, he had also committed an assault resulting from an argument. Roach usually committed crimes for reasons that seemed logical to him. Even the murder seemed logical to Roach, who viewed the victim as a dangerous person who had abused him and various members of his family. Roach told me how upset he had been when someone stole his bicycle and the police kept it for six months before returning it. However, although he felt outraged when his property was stolen, he seemed to have difficulty feeling sorry for his victims.

The School

When I contacted Roach's school, I was surprised that they didn't seem to remember him. Apparently he had been shuffled from school to school — many of his records were not available and few people remembered him. School personnel did remember other children in the family, especially one very bright brother. This neglect points to the problem schools have in maintaining basic information on students. The lack of centralized records resulted in Roach's files being mailed to the latest placement. Roach and his mother weren't even sure where that was. Roach's mother also seemed to have difficulty understanding the various programs and services Roach had received.

The school seemed to have provided Roach and his family with all the services that were available at the time — Chapter 1 reading, special education, and alternative education. Unfortunately, by the time Roach finally reached alternative education, it was too late for him. For his sister, however, Chapter 1 reading had been a successful experience. She explained that it had enabled her to read within the first year.

A School That Could Help

I asked Roach to describe a school that could help a person like him. He said that this was really hard to say, but he would try.

It would be sorta like what I told you alternative school was. First, you wouldn't change rooms for every subject. You would stay in one room. You can get into a lot of trouble when you change rooms and it's confusing. You would have just a few kids in the class — not more than 15 — and two teachers. You need two teachers so that you can get enough help on things you don't understand. In a big class you can't ever get to talk to the teacher alone.

The work would be different too. You would do all your book work in the morning, like reading and social studies and math. You would have science and a computer. I would like to see a computer. I've seen pictures of them, but I would really like to learn how to use one and maybe fix them.

When you did your work, the teachers would show you what it was good for. That was one thing I hated about school. No one ever showed me a use for subtracting. I can see a use for adding, but not subtracting.

After lunch, we would do something creative with our hands. What I am saying is like alternative school. I liked that. I made a doghouse at school. The teacher showed me how to make a blueprint but I threw it away because I wanted to make what I had in my head. But it didn't work; I cut one of the boards too short. The teachers helped me again and it came out right. That doghouse is still standing. I'm in here, but my dog can still sleep in that doghouse.

Death Commuted to Life

Eventually the death sentence was commuted to life in prison by the U.S. Supreme Court because of Roach's age at the time of the crime. At the time of this interview it appeared that Roach would be a prisoner for the rest of his life, unless he could get paroled. He explained how he could work toward being transferred from the maximum security prison to another prison in which he can have more personal freedom. Learning to read and study is one of the ways a prisoner could help himself win that transfer. Recently, Roach won the transfer to another facility, based partly on his success in passing his GED and on his learning to read. It was apparent that Roach was still using the rules of the system to achieve his own goals, even when it meant he had to learn to read.

Roach Learns to Read

During one visit, I asked Roach about his reading. I already knew that he didn't like to write letters because he wasn't sure how to spell all the words. He said that he was learning to read in prison. "When  you are in solitary confinement and can only get out of that cell one hour each day, you will learn how to read. I have been studying for my GED test. If I can get transferred to another prison, they will let me go to school."

It appears then, that Roach was not incapable of learning, but rather that motivation to read had been insufficient for him while in public school. Although no information was available regarding his learning potential, Roach seemed to have been intellectually and physically fit. His major problems seem to be in making logical decisions and evaluating situations from another point of view. Every decision seemed based on his own needs or those of his family.

Roach was very unhappy about having his bike stolen and returned to him damaged by the police six months later. However, it took deliberate leading for him to see that people he had robbed probably felt the same way he did. When I said he "stole" things, he flinched as if I had hit him. He didn't like to think of himself as stealing. He seemed able to hang onto his value system even in prison by renaming the activity. Stealing then, became doing a "job." Assault was "getting even," and murder was "taking care of that character." After our discussion, he admitted that his robbery victims probably felt the same way he had felt when his bike was stolen.

Twisting the Rules

Roach shared some characteristics of the budding criminal. He learned the rules of the school and law system very well, twisting them to serve his own purposes. He knew not to bring drugs to school. Instead, he used them in the neighborhood and on the way to school.

By fourth grade, Roach had learned that he could start a fight, get suspended, and avoid having to read in front of his peers in class. Roach's inability to perform well in front of his peers was an important reason why he wanted to leave school. He said that few of his classmates teased him very much because he beat them up on the playground if they did. It is clear that the embarrassment associated with school was a stronger motivator to leave than any advantage in staying.

Not only did Roach learn to use the rules against the institution, he indicated that kids teach each other how to do it. His small group of buddies taught each other how to stay out of jail by telling authorities anything they wanted to hear. Roach's peer learning was very effective.

Roach said he never lied to his mother, because she wouldn't allow it. However, Roach did not tell her what she didn't know to ask. She didn't think to ask him if he was drinking beer and taking drugs while he was in primary school.

Older brothers and friends are frequently the associates of kids in trouble. His older brothers led the way into trouble for Roach and covered up for him. Even though the parents didn't drink, the older boys kept beer within easy reach of a 6-year-old. The potential of beer as an entry level drug is a controversial issue, but it played an important role in shaping Roach's behavior.

Roach did not like the school system and never seemed to fit in. He recognized this quite early and tried to solve his own problems by skipping school or deliberately getting suspended. He had no reliable assistance in working out his conflicts with the system at school or with the police. His parents did not seem to understand the school programs very well. The school system itself seemed to provoke a conflict situation with his poorly educated family due to the lack of a common language. What seemed to be a logical system to the teachers and principals seemed to the family to be deliberate attempts to put them down or put them into a socially inferior class.

Roach genuinely wanted to solve his own problems and be in control of his own life. Perhaps that is true for many children who are labelled school failures, and we educators would do well to realize that schools do not always have the answers.

Final Thoughts

I was amazed that a person as uneducated as Roach could give a picture of a model school that so closely follows what we know is best in education. The school Roach described would be good not only for him, but for many others like him. The sad thing is that we know how to make good schools but we rarely do so because of tradition and because of legal, control, and money issues. Shortly after Roach was convicted, the alternative education program he attended closed for lack of funds. Only recently have school officials been able to reinstitute the program with special funds.

There was a time when Roach might have jumped on his horse, ridden west, and carved out a future on the frontier. Now, the new frontier is within ourselves and the children who will help to create real schools for real people. We need to study people like Roach to see the gaping holes in the system. Schools built on the efficiency model create a web of rules that are very easy for some students to slip through. Roach found the holes in the system.

When I am very old Roach will still be in prison, an aging reminder that the courts, families, schools, and yes, even children, will need to talk to each other about school in a different way. The design of a good support system for school and community must start with the children themselves.

After six years on death row, Roach passed his GED (general equivalency diploma) and was transferred out of solitary confinement to a minimum security facility. He will not be eligible for parole for many years.

There are allegations that Roach and his siblings may have suffered some sexual and physical abuse.

JULIE, FALLING THROUGH THE CRACKS

Despite Julie's alcoholism, sexual promiscuity, and history of abuse, she was expected to graduate from high school on schedule. At age 17, she had succeeded better in her senior year than she had in the last four years.

Julie attended a medium-sized high school in a rural community. Many of the people who lived there were related to Julie's parents and except for a brief stay with an aunt, Julie had lived there, with her parents, since her birth. Julie had an older sister, aged 22, and a younger sister, aged 10.

Julie attended two different rural grade schools, and although her grades were usually Bs and Cs, Julie was one or two years below grade level in reading comprehension and math. She was an example of a student who fell through the cracks; not deficient enough for an LD [learning disabled] program, but behind grade level enough to have trouble.

Throughout grade school Julie lived with her alcoholic and abusive father and alcoholic mother and had few friends. Although her junior high school experience was successful, she began to have occasional spats with teachers and the principal and to experiment with alcohol and sex. Her grades, however, remained the same and she seemed to be doing well in school despite her learning disabilities.

When she entered the ninth grade Julie began having major problems. She began attending parties with her older cousins, where she drank two to three times a week, to excess on many occasions. Both her parents were having bouts of heavy drinking at this time, and both underwent treatment. They were also undergoing court-ordered counseling because of reported abuse by Julie's father to both his wife and daughter in the fall of 1985.

At school, Julie's troubles began when she started distracting students in the classroom of an older retiring teacher. After she received more than 20 detentions from this teacher, she began disrupting other classes. By the second semester she was having trouble in most classes, skipping school often, being tardy to most classes, and fighting with other girls in school. She had some serious confrontations with other teachers and was suspended from school for nine separate days during the 1985-86 school year. Julie participated in in-school and in-home groups as well as individual alcohol and behavior counseling, but she continued to get into more trouble in school and at home. She received only 2.5 credits that year with a 0.5 grade point average and, in the end, was retained in grade.

Julie's second try at ninth grade was even worse than her first. During the first semester she had a fight with a classmate and got a smoking violation, but she passed all but one class the first semester. She continued to have problems with friends, alcohol, and parents.

Problems at school coupled with a new, more rigorous, discipline policy put Julie in jeopardy of expulsion. A suspension for skipping school also put her at risk of expulsion. In March 1987 she again skipped school, and when told of her impending expulsion, she stormed out of the building shouting a string of obscenities and broke a window worth $125. She was expelled at the end of March, but she was given homebound instruction, an action which enabled her to pass most of her classes and to graduate to the tenth grade.

At home Julie was still having serious problems with her father. In the summer of 1987 she moved to her aunt's house in a small town over 200 miles away. She had trouble in her new school from her parents and after two and a half months her aunt sent her back home. Once back at her old school, Julie improved. She passed all her classes and had very few discipline problems. She was maturing but continued to abuse alcohol and still had problems with her father. At the beginning of the second semester, after numerous counseling sessions with the at-risk coordinator, Julie admitted she still had a dependency problem with alcohol and finally agreed to an assessment and inpatient treatment if necessary. Julie had a two-week evaluation in early February 1988 and entered an eight-week treatment program.

When she returned home Julie had some genuine concerns about her ability to handle negative peer pressure. The school, with advice from the treatment center, put Julie back on homebound instruction for the remainder of the 1987-88 school year.

Again Julie did well and was promoted to eleventh grade, very close to senior status with a good chance of graduating with her class.

During her eleventh and twelfth grade years she stayed out of trouble for the most part; her drinking was somewhat under control, and she was handling problems at home much better. She had one suspension for smoking on a field trip and numerous absences (missing school when she had trouble with her parents, an argument with her girlfriend, or a confrontation with a teacher).

It appeared Julie might pass all her classes and stay on track for graduation. She remained on the edge of quitting school but appeared to be gaining confidence. Her future could have gone either way — good or bad — but her prospects appeared to be improving.

Julie's Personality

Julie was in jeopardy. She became angry when things didn't go her way and she protested she was treated unfairly, even when her behavior was her own fault. She was very unsure of herself in many situations and tried to avoid problems by running away from them. She had difficulty dealing with criticism from other students and preferred to fight than use reason to deal with a given situation. She avoided taking responsibility for her own choices. For example, she chose to miss class or be tardy yet felt unfairly treated when she didn't pass the class.

Julie had a poor self image. She was pretty but thought she was unattractive, especially to boys. She could be a very likeable person and due to her home problems elicited greater flexibility and tolerance from teachers, administrators, counselors, and other adults in her life. She overcame many obstacles, a strength in her personality that people admired. She wanted to continue her education and had so far succeeded academically, despite her below-grade-level work in reading and math.

Julie's relationships with other students had always been limited to very few friends, although she had had one in particular since grade school. She never had had more than two or three friends. Her social life was limited to these few friends and to her cousins, who are older students. She had numerous fights with other girls, usually over boy issues. These often occurred at parties when she was drunk.

Julie had always been very sexually active, sometimes having relations with more than one male in an evening. This practice, although directly tied to her alcoholism, had pigeonholed Julie among her peers as a whore or slut. The behavior of her closest friend since childhood followed a similar pattern: drinking, fighting, skipping class, having trouble in academic performance, promiscuity, and limited friendships. The two friends seemed to rely on each other to the extent that when they argued, neither came to school because they didn't have anyone to talk to. Julie had not dated anyone from her own high school; her partners had either been older boys no longer in school or students from a larger nearby city.

Julie's relationships with teachers were also very erratic. Since her treatment, she seemed to get along with most teachers as long as they were flexible and overlooked her truancy and the acting out of her anger. When dealing with older teachers, especially male teachers, however, she had serious problems. She also had trouble with teachers who graded according to attendance; they informed her that she might fail due to poor attendance and she felt that, again, she was being treated unfairly.

Julie at Home

Julie's relationship with her parents was probably the root of her social problems. Her parents, along with most of her relatives in the area, were heavy drinkers; some were alcoholics. Julie's mother and father both underwent treatment for alcoholism; her mother stayed sober since treatment, but her father still drank excessively.

Most of Julie's conflict occurred with her father. He was reported for physical abuse at least three times. Social service abuse records were not available, but it was suspected that the abuse may have been sexual; there may have been more occurrences than those reported. Julie's father was a transient boilermaker and was often gone for two to three months at a time. Julie hated him and often ran away from home after fights with him.

Julie loved her mother — she was often a great asset to Julie's successes. However, she had a good relationship with her mother only when her father was not at home. When mother and father were together they often drank and made life rough for Julie.

Julie and her younger sister were very close. The sister seemed quite withdrawn, perhaps a normal reaction to all the problems in the home, and Julie said her sister encouraged her not to drink and to be very careful with boys.

When life got difficult, Julie often ran away to her older sister's house, about five miles away. Her sister was married, had children, and was a full-time bartender, a job that figured in Julie's road to alcoholism. Julie also often escaped to parties with the numerous relatives she had in the area. Alcohol was an integral part of people's lives in this rural Finnish community. Julie's extended family (and many other people in the area) seemed to be as involved in excessive drinking as her immediate family.

Julie's future and her successes or failures at home, school, and with friends were all interrelated. As this report was written her life teeters on the brink, and could go in either direction. Her chances of graduating depended on her attendance and class assignments. During her senior year she came to school just enough and did just enough of her assignments in order to remain eligible for graduation. Problems with other students were still present, but she was learning to react less violently and to ask for help when she was angry. At home she still had a poor relationship with her father but planned to move away from her father, even out of the area, after graduation.

Julie at School

School was one stable part of Julie's life. It offered alternatives and interventions in her problems. Classroom teachers made accommodations, although there was some evidence that a few teachers' discipline measures were roadblocks to Julie's success. Tutoring was offered in the high school setting, but Julie thought she didn't need it and that it wouldn't help, despite her earlier success with a remedial class for failed social studies students. Julie was also in a home economics vocational curriculum, which helped her concentrate her efforts and helped her with such classes as teen living and family relations.

The school's at-risk program helped Julie in a number of ways. For example, staff members helped Julie find a job as a bookkeeper on a large farm in the area, where she worked 10 hours a week for minimum wage. The job improved Julie's self-esteem and gave her an opportunity to earn spending money, which her parents had been unable to provide from their low incomes.

Julie was also part of the "work for credit" program during her senior year. She was catching up on required credits by earning one credit working at the same farm and an additional 30 hours of career education, which directed her toward a career as an administrative assistant or cosmetologist. As part of her career education, she also received instruction in job applications and resumes, good work habits, job-seeking skills, payroll deductions, and interviewing.

Through the at-risk program Julie received counseling and alcohol intervention treatment. She had individual counseling in anger control, sexual awareness, drug and alcohol awareness, dealing with parents and peers, and she attended group sessions for alcohol treatment. In early 1988, the at-risk counselor worked with her for a week to help her with her alcohol abuse problem. She finally accepted the fact that she had a problem and agreed to an evaluation and an eight-week treatment. Upon returning from treatment, she received individual help to maintain her sobriety.

The school's at-risk program also helped Julie receive homebound instruction (a teacher instructed her how to pass classes). The first experience came after her expulsion in the spring of 1987. The at-risk program provided the homebound instruction to salvage her second semester grades. Also, after Julie's alcohol treatment, she felt she could not yet function in the school setting under peer pressure. The school again provided homebound instruction to help her complete the second semester credits, which she did successfully. Further changes through the at-risk program kept Julie from teachers she might have had troubles with and classes she might not have been able to pass.

Most of Julie's teachers thought she would be lucky to get a high school diploma, but most liked her and wanted her to attain this goal. Most thought she was fortunate to still be in school and that the school had gone out of its way to assist her. Many teachers thought she had not worked through all of her problems but that she had come a long way since the ninth grade. She was trustworthy for the most part and functioned well in her job. Most adults felt she would probably stay out of major trouble. It appeared she would still have to deal with her alcohol abuse and sexual promiscuity.

Julie's problems were greater than what the school could deal with. For Julie to become a productive member of society, most observers thought she should have continued to receive help after she left school.

Julie completed high school graduation requirements January 27, 1991, completing her last two credits through an at-risk program. She ranked 117th out of 117 in her graduating class, with a 1.04 grade point average. She plans to attend the local technical college and train to be a nurse's assistant. Medication has helped her disposition. She left home recently and now lives with her boyfriend.

Due to the way the state records statistics, Julie has not been counted, back recorded, as a graduate with her senior class because she completed graduation requirements later.

DAVID, GROWING UP ALONE

Like many at-risk students, David fell through bureaucratic cracks. He lacked the right kind of characteristics to make him eligible for intervention programs, yet he was very much at risk.

David's dilemma is a familiar one for children of our era. As the only child of a single parent, he spent large chunks of each day alone. His problems were perhaps more serious than many latchkey children, but his aloneness is a common feature of many children's lives.

David was a survivor. Since age five he had adapted to a life of constant upheaval. His mother had left and his dad worked the evening shift. Except for school hours, David spent most of his time alone; he had learned to get by on his own.

His career plans were characteristic of his attitude of self-sufficiency. He said he wanted to be a jet fighter pilot when he grew up. I asked him if he liked experiences such as riding a roller coaster. He said no, because he had no control on the roller coaster. As a pilot, he said he could run the show.

Unfortunately, David's lifestyle affected his self-control in school. Most nights he stayed awake until midnight, when his father returned from work. His late nights, in turn, affected his ability to stay awake during the day. Not only was he sleeping through most of the school day, he showed little concern for education and no commitment to classroom assignments or responsibilities.

David's father showed little concern for his son's school problems. While to outward appearances the relationship between David and his father seemed one of mutual concern, it was not beneficial to either. David's father did not understand what was developmentally appropriate for a 10-year-old-boy, and David was trying to keep house and prepare meals for a father who worked until nearly midnight.

I asked David how he was doing with grades. He said he was doing well, with the exception of an F in science. His teachers,

43

on the other hand, worried that David would be retained due to poor grades and his inability or unwillingness to complete assignments.

His quick smile and attractive oriental features endeared him to people. He appeared to be average weight and height until he stood next to his classmates, who were somehow more solid. Despite his good looks, David believed he was unattractive. When I asked him how he felt about himself, he stopped talking and hung his head. When I asked David about his friends, he said that he was popular and had a number of friends. School personnel said he was a loner.

David's Day

When the school bus came to his house, David was often still sleeping. When David missed his bus, his father drove him to school, or he walked, or the school principal drove him. When David missed an hour or more of school, he had to make up the time at the end of the day. If David stayed after school, he missed his bus and had to walk home, a distance of several miles.

During the morning at school, David functioned relatively well, although he rarely, if ever, had homework assignments completed. After lunch he found it very difficult to stay awake and missed most of the classroom work.

David arrived home at 3:10 p.m., and on the days his father worked, he was alone until 11:40 p.m. During that time he was not allowed to have neighborhood children in the house. The one exception was Peter, a 12-year-old who occasionally came to visit. During the long hours alone David watched television, played his Nintendo game, or went to the video store for a movie. He was able to fix his own supper.

Most children anticipate special holidays with much excitement and joy. David spent Thanksgiving day alone; his father had to work. During Christmas vacation he flew to visit relatives.

David's days flowed one into another in an unbroken river of monotony, loneliness, and insecurity.

David at School

"We all have sad feelings sometimes, don't we?" asked the fourth-grade health teacher, trying to evoke some class discussion of the unit "Knowing Ourselves and Others Better." As some students eagerly talked about their emotions, David appeared to slump, his head resting on his arm, elbow on the desk. It was 1:00 p.m., the time when David found it most difficult to remain attentive or even awake.

David Grossman

The teacher tried to elicit a response from David. "It helps to talk to people about our feelings, doesn't it?" she queried, sneaking glances David's way. By now his eyes had closed and his head kept alternately drooping and jerking up. By 1:30 p.m. David had lost the battle to stay awake and was sleeping soundly with his nose flat against the desk.

At this point a student sitting close by announced, "David, wake up." David groggily lifted his head and stared straight ahead, glassy-eyed. "Class," the teacher began, "I would like you to take out a piece of paper and write 'I am likable because. . . .' Then list the reasons you think your friends and classmates like you." David didn't move. "David did you get out a piece of paper yet?" asked his teacher. David fumbled in his desk for some paper and pencil but made no attempt to comply with the request.

Within minutes he was sleeping again. The student sitting next to David looked over and said quietly, "David's tired." By 1:35 p.m. David did not try to hide his condition or shake himself awake. He was fast asleep.

At 1:45 p.m. the social studies teacher, who is also David's primary teacher (homeroom and math as well) entered the room and asked the students to take out their books and notebooks. David woke up and asked to go to his locker and get his book. The movement seemed to shake him from his stupor, although his initial involvement in the discussion was minimal and he appeared to be sleeping with his eyes open.

Finally, when the class began to discuss violent types of weather, David came to life, excited to talk about a typhoon in Japan. Before he could drift off again, the teacher asked, "David, what is fertile soil?" He paused, thought, and responded, "Good for growing plants." There was a slight pause before the teacher acknowledged that his answer was correct. At that point a broad grin appeared on his face, and he audibly sighed with relief. Now David was awake and began waving his hands in response to further questions.

This scene was typical in David's life. Falling asleep was certainly a problem and contributed (as either cause or effect) to his complete lack of motivation to perform any schoolwork either in class or at home. The fact that his intellectual abilities did not warrant any special assistance, class placement, or even an Individual Education Plan, made his case particularly sad.

David's teachers worried about his situation and tried to express their concern to both David and his father. On two occasions they met with David's father. Each time the father said he wanted to change the situation. The faculty felt very positive about his assertions, but eventually questioned his abilities and desire to follow through.

David's teachers began sending a daily assignment form home with him, asking his father to sign it when the work was done. He signed the forms regardless of whether work had been completed.

David's teachers also telephoned and visited his father to remind him to provide the necessary follow-through on problems. One evening, at a local high school football game, one of David's teachers watched him racing around and yet never connecting with an individual or a group. He had been absent from school that day and so the teacher confronted David's father about his absence from school and subsequent presence at the ball game. The father became defensive and refused to discuss the issue.

Several times David had arrived at school with wet hair and one time, a bloody nose. The three times he was picked up by the principal, he had to stay after school to make up the time missed in the morning. One morning he walked to school, arriving at 10 a.m.

David occasionally complained of stomachaches. He often appeared exhausted, unmotivated, unorganized, and irresponsible. His primary teacher hugged him every day, but David never responded in any visible manner. However, he never showed any disrespect for any faculty members.

When winter came and the ground was wet, David had no boots. Teachers spoke to both David and his father several times about boots and received no response. The teachers insisted he wear a pair of used boots when he was at school. This demand seemed to motivate David to persuade his father to provide him with boots. The family was not poor, and David wore stylish tennis shoes and jeans.

David's teachers also worried that he would be retained due to failing grades. They were not sure whether David and his father understood the implications of such an action. Incidents like these finally prompted the school staff to build a case for either inappropriate parenting skills or neglect. They worked with David within the school system structure, but they also documented the rationale for intervention by social services.

Teachers called on David often when he was attentive enough to raise his hand. During one math lesson David was forced to sit in the hallway during the beginning of the lesson while the other students went over some homework that he had not completed. When he was able to enter the class, he was eager to be called upon. However, when the direction was given to put down pencils and watch the blackboard, David did not comply. At that point the teacher came to his desk, touched him, and whispered that he needed to be paying attention to her. The interaction, like many others throughout the day, was very positive.

David had few friends, but he did not seem concerned. This lack of friends was not due, as is commonly true, to antisocial behavior, but rather to his omission of appropriate behavior. Whether cause or effect, David's desire to remain indoors during recess kept him from making friends. While he was not a shy child, he also was not aggressive and did not seek out peers. Rarely did a classmate choose to work with him on a project.

David perceived that he was well accepted and had numerous friends. Observations and teacher reports presented a very different picture. While David was not aggressively rejected, neither was he included. Rather he seemed to be ignored, as peers viewed him as somewhat of a silent partner, a classmate who lacked motivation and slept his way through the day. I did not determine whether David's perception about his popularity was one of denial or a misconception.

Conclusions

David's situation was frustrating because he could not be categorized. Professionals assign students at risk due to low IQ or developmental delays to special classrooms or Chapter I teachers. Students at risk because of substance abuse are provided appropriate treatment. Students who are victims of abuse or obvious neglect are placed in foster care. Students with behavior problems are assigned management aides or placed in special classrooms. David fit in none of these categories, yet he was clearly failing to do his school work.

Does something as intangible as instability lead to failure? David had moved almost yearly since age four and a half. Does inadequate nurturing lead to failure? Although he had spent some summers with his mother, David lived with a father who, for whatever reasons, did not provide appropriate nurturing for a young boy. Perhaps the family's attitude was at fault. Father and son were not concerned, because David had made it through four years of school. Nevertheless, the results of his lifestyle — physical exhaustion, ennui, lack of motivation, disorganization, inability to relate to others, unrealistic perceptions — certainly threatened to spell failure.

David's presence in class was never disruptive or time-consuming; his absence would probably have gone unnoticed. David's transformation from a cipher to a child with untapped potential might happen soon; it might never happen. Situations like David's pose many questions, but the answers are few.

———

David and his father left the school district in the spring following this study. The school's principal assumes their departure was due to a combination of pressure from school personnel and the search for different employment.

JOSÉ, SENSITIVE AND MERCURIAL

José at Home

José's eyes sparkled and he smiled broadly as he talked about sports. Several years ago he wanted to be a truck driver. Last year he said he wanted to be a football player. But José didn't participate in school- or community-sponsored activities because his family could not afford the uniforms, dues, and transportation.

The fourth-grade teachers in his public elementary school in the Southwest selected José, a 10-year-old Hispanic, as most at-risk because of his behavioral problems, their experiences with him in the classroom, and their interviews with his mother. Transfer records were available from the school he had attended in the second grade, but no records could be obtained from the school he attended in the first grade. In addition, no counseling records existed, even though José met with the school counselor regularly for over a year.

The family lived in a three-bedroom, modestly furnished home. Over the years, an increasing number of public housing units had been built in the once largely middle-class neighborhood. José's mother, a single parent, did not work outside the home and received money from Aid to Families with Dependent Children (AFDC) to help support José, his older brother, and younger sister. The family was unaware of services and facilities for the children, and their social involvement in the new community was minimal.

José was friendly, good looking, stylish, and smiled often. Although he was a bit smaller than most children his age, he held his own with his older brother and friends. He and his brother often played at wrestling, using holds learned from television and magazines. Their mother believed this behavior spilled over to school — José often got in trouble for fighting with other students. José said that at school he was just "messing around," as he did with his brother and close friends.

José's Family

José loved and respected his mother, and she felt concern for her children. She said José did not know his biological father and that he had made no attempt to see José. The only father José had known was his stepfather, who married José's mother when he was one year old. The marriage produced José's sister, but also ended in divorce. José's mother said she divorced her second husband because he had abused her. She claimed he had not abused the children.

When we interviewed José he had not seen his stepfather for three months. Unconfirmed reports suggested he might have been jailed on drug-related charges. About three weeks after the initial interview, the stepfather returned for a short visit. José told a fourth-grade teacher that during the visit the stepfather assaulted his mother. José said he tried to defend her with a makeshift weapon. However, he denied the story when asked by a school interview team. Apparently, violence continued in the home despite José's unwillingness to admit it.

José seemed very attached to his stepfather, and teachers mistakenly thought he was José's biological father. José told his teachers that his stepfather wrote to him and sent him drawings. I wondered if José's positive feelings toward his stepfather were a fantasy.

José was very protective of his younger sister. He waited for her after school, watched over her, and gave her money if she needed it. However, he frequently fought with his older brother, who often made fun of him and called him names because he attended special reading classes. His mother said she would often hear her older son call José a "retard." However, quarrels among the three children appeared to occur no more than in other families.

José had a 16-year-old uncle who communicated with him about twice a month. The boys admired their uncle, who, according to José, gave them positive feedback. He told José not to let others call him names and to do whatever he must to defend himself.

José often saw his extended family. At Christmas, he visited his grandparents and often received some of the presents on his wish list. The family members were substitutes for the friends most children had in such a community.

The third-grade teacher said that when José had attended her class he was unable to make friends and started fights outside the classroom; some students had continued to call him names because he attended special classes. However, she thought that as a fourth-grader he got along better with the other children. He smiled more often and was better able to hold his temper. Last year, José passed the necessary exit test and was no longer in special classes. The name calling from his brother and others stopped and José appeared to have better self-esteem.

José's fourth-grade teacher said that he used to force himself on his peers and was unable to work effectively within a group. Instead, the teacher often worked with him alone. The few classmates José hung around with were frequently those much like himself — students labeled quarrelsome troublemakers.

José had established good rapport with the head custodian, an Hispanic male. Except for the uncle, the custodian was the only positive male role model in José's life.

José at School

José attended preschool for only a few months. His mother said she had had trouble picking him up on time because she worked, so she took him out of school. He went directly to first grade, probably starting school socially and academically behind the other children in his class. The family had moved several times and José had attended three different schools.

There was no information in José's folder regarding first-grade academic work. However, records indicated that in second grade he had a B average in math, social studies, science, art, music, and physical education, but was below level in reading. He withdrew from the second grade 16 days before the end of the school year, but was admitted into his current school and completed the remaining school year there.

The home language survey indicated that English was the language José spoke most of the time in the home, which was confirmed through interview and observations. During José's third-grade year, he maintained a B average in math, science, and social studies, but was placed in a reading resource class because he continued to read below his grade level. The results of a state-mandated basic skills test indicated mastery of minimum grade-three competencies in mathematics, reading, and writing. However, he scored below the twentieth percentile in reading on the Metropolitan Achievement Test.

The third-grade teacher reported that José tested at the first-grade reading level. He was unmotivated, and his attention span was very short, although attention deficit disorder was ruled out as a problem. Further observations indicated possible problems at home. At times he would be hostile and defensive, perhaps because he needed to put up defenses to survive. At the beginning of the school year he would often display aggressive behavior in class, but his teacher told him it was not necessary and he eased off after a while. José confided to his teacher that both his stepfather and his uncle told him to show others that he would not allow himself to be shoved around. The third-grade teacher stressed that although he displayed a macho attitude, he was nevertheless very fragile, sensitive, and needed much love and reassurance.

The school counselor learned that José was suffering emotionally, and was able to build some trust and rapport with him. The counselor told one teacher that José was one of the students most in need of counseling. Although the mother had some reservations about counseling at first, she became supportive of it after being reassured that it was in the best interest of her son. She also supported José's placement in remedial reading.

The third- and fourth-grade teachers said that by the end of the third grade José's self-concept had improved, although he still had a long way to go. Observations during fourth grade indicated that he seemed to be getting along better with classmates and did not seem to get into as much trouble. Both teachers kept in contact with him. They thought it was important to continue to work closely with José and his family throughout the school year and to provide him with as many positive comments as possible.

José in the Classroom

José spent his school day like most other pupils. The homeroom teacher presented some lessons, but other teachers provided other lessons. Selected interactions of a typical school day for José in fourth grade follow.

In the health class, the teacher asked the students to write five reasons why marijuana should be legal or five reasons why it should not be legal. Although José didn't mention drug use by the family, peers, or himself, he did reveal an awareness of the harm that drugs can cause.

José went to another class to receive special help in reading. José did a fair job of reading the passages aloud. Often, he read better than the other three in the group. At one point, he even corrected another student who mispronounced a word. He was ready with an answer to almost all of the teacher's questions.

Although José was generally paying attention while we observed him, the reading teacher later revealed that he was usually disruptive and was apathetic about answering the questions. In an earlier interview, José revealed that he found the reading class boring and thought he did better than the other kids. A few weeks later, perhaps as a result of this study, José was placed in a higher reading level and began receiving reading resource instruction with a group of fifth-graders.

José's instructional experiences in science and language arts were also videotaped but did not reveal any significant information. Perhaps the initial presence of the camera inhibited teacher and student behaviors of importance to this case study.

José's Teachers

The fourth-grade teacher explained that her resource program was called a magnet classroom, where a low student-teacher ratio was maintained. Students assigned to such classrooms were often in trouble, on medication, functioning at a low academic level, or exhibiting maladaptive social behavior or attention deficit disorder. Some high achievers were assigned to this class to provide balance. Teachers received no special training for teaching these students, but, in theory, the low student-teacher ratio allowed the teacher time to work more closely with each student.

I asked her why she thought that José was considered to be more at-risk than other students. She replied that he brought his problems to school, could not cope with major problems, and got violent when things did not go well. She described José as a "time bomb ready to explode."

Regular methods of discipline didn't seem to work with him. However, she said he did respond when she took extra care with him. As she got to know him better she was more able to identify his problems. She stressed, however, that such attention was not always possible, because she also had other students in need of her attention. Nonetheless, he maintained a C average with her.

The fourth-grade teacher found José had a low self-concept and was very sensitive. He cried around adults, although not with his peers or other students. He learned from an early age that physical violence was a viable answer. He was not taught to respect his elders and obey rules.

The teacher met with his mother on occasion and found her to be very intelligent and a very caring person who seemed to want what was best for her children. She thought that José needed to have a consistent person in his life whom he could trust, and that a positive male role model probably would be an asset. She explained that the school counselor's intervention in 1987-88 was very beneficial to José. She believed continued counseling would improve his academic progress and emotional well-being. She suggested that José be assigned to just one counselor who could follow his progress throughout the critical school years ahead. That year, the school had a female counselor who was attractive and youthful looking. She said José had not been to visit her, although she maintained an open-door policy much like the previous counselor's.

Although José received most classes from the homeroom teacher, other teachers went to his homeroom to teach health, English, and science. We had interviews with José's health and English teachers, but the science teacher did not wish to be interviewed.

The health teacher described José as a "nice little boy" who would try very hard during instruction. She said she had no particular behavior problems with him and that he usually paid attention and provided her with reasons if he was absent. He did have some weaknesses in reading and spelling, and although he had as much opportunity to participate as the rest of the class, he hardly ever raised his hand to answer. She frequently found herself pulling information from him.

The physical education teacher indicated that José was a natural athlete who excelled in sports. When asked about José's aggressive behavior, he indicated that José did not fight any more than the average student in his class.

The remedial teacher, who also taught José language arts and math, described José's behavior in her classes as variable. She said sometimes "he was a very nice and well-mannered little boy." However, at times he was very hard to work with; he would become uncooperative and disruptive. She described his disruptive behavior as "undermining and sneaky." For example, he would kick the other kids, throw things on the sly, and "yell and say ugly words." José befriended a student who became his companion in mischief. During the videotaping, José made signals to the student sitting next to him, which resulted in their throwing spit wads at each other. The teacher did not notice. He smiled then laughed nervously when he realized the camera had recorded the incident.

The teacher described José's self-image as very low and said that he perceived himself as a failure. She said he was reading at the third-grade level, like the other students in his group. However, he was reading at a much lower level in 1987-88.

In 1989-90 José was again placed in reading resource class with a new teacher. She had several conferences with him about the importance of completing class assignments and trying hard in reading class. The time and patience she devoted to him apparently paid off. According to José's fifth-grade teacher, José's work was just about on a par with most of his classmates. Also, José just recently had passed the tests necessary to be released from reading resource. He seemed to have a better attitude about himself, although he still managed to get into trouble when it came to horseplay with other students.

José's Parents

When José's mother was interviewed two months after he started fourth grade, she said that she didn't know his teacher that well and that she had difficulty talking with her. She claimed that the teacher told her one thing and José told her something else. She cited an incident that occurred when José had returned to school after having been absent for a few days. The school held a science fair, she said, during the last period of the day. José told his mother that the teacher had said, "Now you know what you're going to do while we go." José thought she meant he had to remain alone in the classroom and could not attend the science fair in the auditorium with the other students. When the teacher returned to the classroom, having dismissed the class for the day in the auditorium, she found José still sitting in the classroom. She asked José why he had not attended the fair. He yelled at her, and was immediately sent to the principal's office. However, his mother said that the teacher denied telling José he couldn't attend the fair. The mother considered the incident a confidential matter, but later discovered that the teacher had discussed it with other teachers.

The mother talked with the teacher to have her understand José better. She told the teacher that José responded well to people who showed patience and understanding. She said that José was more likely to do something if he knew the reason behind it; simply telling him not to do it didn't work. She said he would also "close up if you are short with him or if he feels you are upset with him."

José's mother was cautiously optimistic about his immediate future in school. She thought his success "depended on whether the teachers would take the time to notice José's problems and needs."

Summary, Recommendations and Prognosis

The most significant at-risk factors for José in 1990 were exposure to violence in the home and lack of continuous, positive adult contact, particularly with male role models. Other factors included negative feelings toward being in a reading resource class and lack of consistent counseling. In 1990, José left the reading class and a permanent counselor was assigned to the school, should José need her services.

I thought it was essential for José and his family to receive counseling. I also recommended the school officials seek help from social agencies to improve the home situation.

In addition, José should be provided with a part-time tutor to help him continue to improve his reading. The stable presence of supervisory and counseling personnel was essential for José.

Teachers often viewed events and situations at home through the eyes of José. Similarly, the mother's perceptions of school events were filtered through José. Therefore, in some circumstances, teachers probably did not accurately assess José's problems, a situation that sometimes led to the wrong prescriptions. For example, teachers suggested that José's stepfather (who may have influenced José's aggressive behavior) be more involved in his life.

Vital information on José, such as academic progress and counseling sessions, should be transmitted from one school to another and from one set of teachers to another so that the academic and emotional needs of José are not overlooked. Otherwise, José may "fall through the cracks" as he moves from one grade to another, particularly as he makes the transition to junior high school, where school personnel will not have direct access to previous instructors.

José has an excellent chance of succeeding in school and in life if his progress continues to be monitored and active steps are taken to continue meeting his academic and emotional needs.

José is now twelve years old. He attends the same school, although his classes are now taught by six different teachers. He no longer takes remedial reading, even though he does borderline work as a C student. His behavior has improved, but he continues to act up with certain teachers. He gets sent to the office about once or twice a week for "talking back." His home situation has not changed; his mother is still a single parent.

WILLIE, BETWEEN SHY AND TALKATIVE

Willie was quick to smile, pleasant, and cooperative. He spoke freely about his experiences at home and school, where he was a 16-year-old tenth-grader at the local school for ninth- and tenth-graders.

Although he was somewhat awkward with adults, Willie was respectful and used acceptable manners. He seemed more awkward with people his own age and was to some extent a loner. His activities outside school did not include people his own age, and his speech, actions, and appearance set him apart from the other students. He did not have many friends and once explained that the reason for this was "I couldn't remember all their names anyway." He described himself as "sort of between shy and talkative."

Willie was tall (approximately 5'11"), and he weighed about 180 pounds. His clothes were unfashionable and too small; his pants ended above his ankles, his T-shirts were tight, and his jacket sleeves didn't reach his wrists. His hair had a slight natural curl and was cut short. He had a sparse growth of beard, a blemish-free, and a very fair complexion. He wore dark-framed glasses, which he habitually pushed up with an index finger.

Since his mother's death six years before the interview and his father's imprisonment 10 years before that, Willie had lived as an only child with his maternal grandparents, his mother's older sister, and her husband. He had two younger half-brothers, but he had not seen them since his mother's death. No one in Willie's family had ever graduated from high school, but they all encouraged Willie's efforts to graduate.

There were about 18,000 people in Willie's small town, approximately 100 miles from the nearest metropolitan city. The local school district had about 2,500 students in seven elementary schools, one middle school (seventh and eighth grades), a mid-high school (ninth and tenth grades), one senior high school (eleventh and twelfth grades), and a vocational-technical school for senior high students.

Willie at Home

Willie's family had limited income, consisting of social security benefits and a small amount from Willie's part-time, minimum-wage job. The family paid $62 a month rent for a small, white, wood-frame, six-room house in an old, low-income area. The small, neat rooms were arranged so that one had to go through each room to get to the next. One room was a converted one-car garage. There were no interior doors, except to the bathroom. The modest, older furniture, mostly from the 1950s and 60s, was lined up along the walls of each room.

The livingroom opened through an archway directly into Willie's room. The arrangement didn't permit much privacy, but Willie was proud of his room and the way he had decorated it with his collection of baseball caps, American flags, and a large rebel flag. On his double bed was a Star Wars comforter and a handmade quilt. Trophies and memorabilia filled a small shelf. A lamp, several books, papers, and a small amount of clutter adorned his desk, which his grandfather had made for him. A dresser and a small table with a stereo radio and record player in one unit stood nearby.

The family did not own a car, and Willie did not have a driver's license or driving permit. Willie had a ten-speed bicycle, which he kept in his room, and his grandfather had rebuilt an older bicycle that he and Willie's aunt sometimes rode.

The slight, 76-year-old grandfather said he was in good health. He hadn't been sick since he had the "World War I flu," but he tended to ramble and reminisce. He had an eighth-grade education, but had received vocational technical training and had been an aircraft mechanic for a number of years. He had wanted to continue his public school education beyond the eighth grade, but had to quit school and go to work as his own "sole support." He had cried when he couldn't continue his schooling. He was very supportive of Willie's efforts to continue his education and said the family tried to leave Willie alone while he was doing school work. He also said that Willie was smarter than he and could make something out of himself if he really wanted to.

Willie's grandmother said that he had been with her since he was born. She was proud of Willie and said she had enjoyed every minute she had had him. Willie had been a good boy, she said, and listened to her requests most of the time. She had a sixth-grade education and regretted her lack of education. She had supported herself by doing laundry and babysitting. She had diabetes, which affected her vision and general health. When her health failed, the local department of human services had paid for a home-care provider, who worked in the home for three hours a day, cleaning the house, cooking meals, and performing other housekeeping tasks.

Willie's grandmother told him how important it was for him to go to school and get his education, so he could "make something of himself." She felt bad when Willie began to have trouble in school, but she never questioned his ability to complete his education. She believed the school would do whatever was necessary to help him make it through. She also thought the high school counselor cared about Willie and would help him get back into school.

Willie's aunt, who dropped out of school in the tenth grade, had the most education in the family. She got married at age 15, had a baby, and quit school. Willie felt closest to his aunt. He trusted her more than anyone else. He said that if there was anything that he wanted to talk about, but wanted kept confidential, she would respect his wishes.

Willie's aunt assumed much of the responsibility for his care, such as washing his clothes, getting him up for school, and preparing his meals. She had lived with or near Willie most of his life. His aunt said she loved Willie like he was her own son. Her natural son was 30 years old, married, and had a 6-year-old son. Willie's aunt said that her son, "did not get his education and has had a hard time making it." The only information offered about her husband was that they were not getting along.

Willie's aunt had helped him get his part-time job at the local newspaper. According to his grandmother and aunt, Willie considered his job important. His grandmother boasted that Willie's boss said he could do just about anything at work.

Willie kept the part-time job for more than two years. He did not attend school during the second semester of his sophomore year. Both his aunt and his employer tried to get Willie back in school. They went to the school and talked with the administration to ensure that Willie could get back into school. Willie's employer told him he must go back to school and that his job was secure as long as he stayed in school.

Willie's Social Life

Willie began school two weeks after the fall semester started. Shortly after he started school, Willie met Cindy. She was his only girlfriend. She was an attractive, intelligent, 15-year-old sophomore. Cindy was the daughter of Baptist missionaries who had recently returned to the United States from the Philippines. Cindy had never gone to public school before that year. She encouraged Willie to stay in school and graduate. Sometimes Cindy helped Willie with his homework.

Willie attended the same Baptist church as Cindy and helped her deliver papers after school. He earned a small amount of extra money doing this. Cindy's mother had treated Cindy and Willie to lunch at a local restaurant buffet as an extra thanks for his help. Willie benefited socially from his friendship with Cindy and even attended a few ball games with her.

Willie showed little interest in extracurricular activities such as school events, parties, movies, or dances. When he was not working or at school, he stayed at home and watched TV with his grandparents. He enjoyed football and was a strong supporter of his favorite team. He called himself a die-hard fan. He also liked country music, although he didn't play it much.

Some of his leisure time was spent playing video games and pinball machines at a local convenience store. After he played pinball, Willie often went across the street to talk with a man who worked at a service station. Football was the main topic of conversation. If they had an extra dollar, they might bet on an "important" ball game.

Willie did not drink alcohol. He did smoke cigarettes, but seemed self-conscious about it. He smoked at home without restrictions; both of his grandparents chewed tobacco. Willie was not even inclined to try drugs. He did not think he was missing out on anything and felt that his life was interesting.

Willie at School

Willie attended the same school district throughout his education, going to the local neighborhood school during his elementary years. Willie went to both Head Start and kindergarten. During the first grade he had some difficulty, although his report cards for the first grade were incomplete. At the end of the first semester, he received a grade of N (needs improvement) in mathematics, reading, and spelling. The only grade recorded for the second semester was an S plus (S = satisfactory) in mathematics. His first-grade teacher thought that Willie had a large vocabulary, but that he didn't seem to understand specific questions. He received speech therapy in the first grade, but the records are incomplete. He made progress during speech therapy and this helped his reading and spelling performance.

During second semester of the first grade, Willie was evaluated because his teacher was concerned about unsatisfactory classroom performance and low scores on a first-grade test. The evaluation revealed that Willie possessed the academic skills to succeed in school. In fact, he scored above grade level in reading, arithmetic, and spelling. His performance on the Wide Range Achievement Test generated grade-level scores of 1.8 in reading, 2.3 in spelling, and 2.6 in arithmetic. He, also, obtained an average visual-motor age score on the Bender Visual Motor Gestalt Test.

The diagnostician who performed the assessment recommended that Willie be referred for further evaluation by a school psychologist. No reason was given regarding the need for additional information, and there is no record of a referral or other indication that suggests the school district pursued this recommendation.

Willie didn't remember much about his early schooling, but spoke very warmly about his third-grade teacher. He said he really loved her and that she was very thoughtful and took the time to explain things to him so he could understand them. Coincidentally, he began to perform better in third grade. For the first semester he made S pluses in art, social studies, writing, and spelling. His grades improved even more by the second semester. He received an H (excellent, the highest grade) in writing and an H minus in mathematics, language arts, and spelling.

His grades were satisfactory for the fourth and fifth grades. Willie's mother died during the summer between his fourth and the fifth grades. He said he couldn't remember anything about this time of his life, except a big graduation celebration at the end of the fifth grade. In middle school (grades six through eight), Willie received a B average. There were no indications of problems, academically or behaviorally, during that time. Willie said he worked really hard to make good grades during middle school so he could be a library aide. He thought it was an interesting job and enjoyed helping students find books and all the rest of his duties in the library.

His achievement throughout school, as measured by normed achievement tests, was consistently in the average or above-average ranges in all areas. His total achievement composite ranged from the 54th to the 72nd percentile as compared to national norms. Willie said that he enjoyed mathematics. He had a national percentile rank of 97 in the ninth grade. He had difficulty with language arts, although his scores were in the average range.

Willie maintained a B average during his freshman year at the mid-high school. Often students were required to take classes at the senior high school about two miles away. Willie's drama class was at the high school and to attend this class he had to ride the shuttle bus between the two campuses.

Willie said he hadn't cared much for most of his teachers when he began the tenth grade. He thought they didn't take the time he needed for explanation or instruction; they just "threw the work at you." At this time his grandmother became seriously ill and required hospitalization. During this period, when he did attend school, Willie said he was so worried about his grandmother he was unable to concentrate.

Willie and his grandmother both thought that part of Willie's problems at school his first sophomore year had involved a severe personality clash with some of his teachers. Willie started the tenth grade again. He said that he had some problems in English and world history courses. Coincidentally, Willie had the same English teacher he had had a personality clash with the year before. The English teacher declined to participate in this study. The only information provided was a grade of C for the first semester of English II.

Willie thought that world history should be an elective and not a required subject. The material was not interesting to him and he didn't want to know about foreign countries. He thought there was also a personality problem with this teacher, basically because the teacher did not explain material and expected Willie to work out any problems on his own. The world history teacher also declined participation in the study. A grade of F was reported for the first semester in this course.

Physical education was not one of Willie's personal favorites. He didn't appear to get much physical exercise. He did not enjoy the activities, particularly tumbling, and admitted that he did not take part very often. The PE teacher did not wish to participate in the interview, saying he did not know the student. Willie got an F in PE.

Willie liked math and did not have any complaints about Algebra I. He got a B at the end of the first semester. Due to the nonparticipation of the PE, English, and algebra teachers, information about the classroom situation or teaching methods was unavailable, except as revealed by Willie. His schedule was changed second semester and he did not have these same teachers.

Willie's drama teacher was very encouraging and willing to help in any way he could. In the drama classroom there were five desks and chairs, a teacher's desk, and two blackboards. On one of the blackboards was an exceptional piece of artwork done in colored chalk, on the other were reminders of assignments and helpful hints. Shelves along one wall held various objects that could be used as props or catalysts for skits or scenes. The teacher had had the floor carpeted and the desks removed to provide space for the groups to work out their skits.

There was no set curriculum for the drama class; the teacher set up the program using his own ideas, information, and texts. He also encouraged students to write their own scenes, skits, and improvisations. His primary instructional technique involved group participation (with rotating membership), along with demonstration, individual direction, and instruction, combined with peer tutoring. Sometimes when Willie was assigned to a group someone would roll their eyes up, but Willie was soon accepted by the group. The other students in the class generally made an extra effort to include Willie.

The drama teacher encouraged creativity on the part of the students. He thought that Willie had creativity and talent and said "sometimes it just comes bubbling out of him." The drama teacher thought that when Willie came to class, he added to the classroom experience. The teacher said Willie had made progress during the year and had produced at least one exceptional script. The teacher liked how Willie improvised in scenes, particularly his Ed Norton character adapted from "The Honeymooners" (Willie's favorite television comedy).

The drama teacher felt that Willie's strengths involved creativity and that he was capable of being an integral part of the class.

He also was responsible for meeting assignment deadlines. Willie's personal weakness was attendance. He said Willie really wanted to act, which was a plus for his attitude in class. The teacher regretted that Willie had not come to class enough, which had resulted in an incomplete grade for the first semester. Willie was given an opportunity to make up the missed work.

The drama teacher thought that for Willie to graduate, he was going to need a lot of help from his other teachers. He would particularly need help in basic areas such as English and history. He felt that Willie would not have all the self-motivation that he needed, that it might have been driven out of him before he had reached this level.

Willie also took biology. That classroom contained desks, chairs, and some lab tables; the school did not have a traditional biology lab. Dissections or other experimental procedures took place in the classroom. The curriculum materials included textbooks and workbooks, which the teacher supplemented with puzzles, games, and other motivating materials to reinforce lecture information. The class was evaluated using tests, quizzes, homework, lab assignments, and special-interest projects. The curriculum and presentation techniques (lectures, films, individual instruction) were modified to fit the individual students, if necessary.

The biology teacher thought that Willie was intelligent and caring. Willie had never been a problem in class, behaviorally or otherwise. He was conscientious and exact in his work, paying close attention to details. Willie's strengths involved completing his work, being attentive in class, and trying to do the best that he could. Willie often came to class just to talk with his teacher, and sometimes he would carry things into the building for her. Willie was always polite and considerate. His teacher had seen growth in Willie's social skills over the last two years, and the other students had begun accepting Willie more. His teacher specifically attributed his new found self-confidence to his relationship with his girlfriend, Cindy.

Willie had missed 27 days of school in the first semester and this absence contributed to his grade of C. His biology teacher stated that Willie often was slow to respond to questions and discussions in class. He often had to stop in the middle of a sentence to gather his thoughts or to find the right words to say. She thought that he had the potential to graduate, and hoped that he would stay in school. She also thought Willie would need extra motivation and encouragement from his teachers. She expressed concern for Willie, since he had changed classes at the end of the first semester. She hoped that Willie's new biology teacher would take the time to give Willie what he needed. She also thought that the school system could help Willie and keep him in school.

The principal made himself available to the students and teachers at any time. He was firm, but soft-spoken. The principal listened to both sides of a story and was very fair. The principal said he did not really know Willie, but there were two things he knew for sure — Willie had social problems, he looked and dressed different, and Willie's attendance had been a serious problem. The principal thought that the illness of Willie's grandmother had been a major factor in Willie's absentee rate. Willie had not taken his grandmother's illness well. One day the principal had had to take Willie home because he was so upset about his grandmother. The principal said that Willie had never been a problem at school.

Programs for At-Risk Students

When asked what the school system was doing to help at-risk students, the principal replied that the public school system offered an Extended Day Program, which gave students who had failed the required number of classes the opportunity to make up those credits. Students could take two classes from the Extended Day Program. Classes began at 4:00 p.m. and 5:00 p.m. and were held four days a week. Each student had to attend class for 75 hours to receive credit. An independent study contract was required of all students in the Extended Day Program.

The public school system had also implemented an Achievement Action Program in order to better meet the needs of the at-risk student population. The goal of this program was to increase the opportunities for success of those students who traditionally underachieved or were in danger of dropping out of school. The general objectives of the Achievement Action Program were to

- increase parental and community involvement
- increase parental and teacher expectations for student academic achievement

- develop and enhance instructional strategies for student differences
- promote a positive self-concept in students
- develop and enhance administrative leadership for change

The system also had a peer tutoring program, in which any student could receive tutelage for one hour before and after school, and a mentor program in the senior high, in which a teacher followed the progress of a student. The teacher took a personal interest in that student, providing support and encouragement. The school system was also seeking funding for an alternative school program, which was in the planning stages.

The tenth-grade counselor was caring, personable, and consistent in her efforts to help students succeed in school. She often went beyond regular school hours to encourage students. The counselor worked with Willie to find out his specific needs and to develop a program that would suit him. The counselor appeared to have taken a personal interest in Willie. She found more appropriate clothes for him so he would fit in better at school, and she had improved communication between the school and his family. The counselor had known Willie for three years and said that Willie seemed consumed with concern about his grandmother. Willie said if anything happened to her he wouldn't have anyplace to go and wouldn't know what to do.

The counselor thought that Willie's relationship with Cindy helped keep him in school and had a positive influence on his social relationships with other children. There were times when Cindy acted as a go-between. She would tell the counselor when Willie wasn't in school. The counselor would ask Cindy to call Willie and tell him to get to school — no excuses. Willie would come to school after Cindy called him.

The counselor was concerned that Willie might not finish school. She said that he certainly had the capability, as shown by his achievement scores (which were between the 54th and 72nd percentile). She noted that Willie had some personality problems with some of his teachers. She also mentioned that Willie was "different," with out-of-style clothes and a unique character. There were other students similar to Willie, but they didn't fit in either.

The counselor spoke about how Willie was a special, loving person. He appeared to be caring and had helped her carry things up the stairs. On one occasion Willie was feeling bad and she told him he was special and did things to help other people. It wasn't long after that that she walked downstairs past the special education classroom and Willie was there helping students. He had made a habit of going in there and helping students. Willie told her "Yes, I guess, I can help people." The counselor thought that Willie would make a good contribution to society and would try his best at any job. She said next year Willie would be in computer classes at the vocational-technical school.

As indicated by family and educators, Willie was not strongly motivated to complete school. His ability to achieve academically was not questioned; he had already displayed that. Yet, some teachers expressed surprise when Willie would make an exemplary effort.

Socially, Willie didn't fit in with many other students. The only peer he talked with regularly at school was his girlfriend. However, our interview was pleasant. Willie did not display discomfort or uneasiness in a one-to-one situation − either when we were in his home or in the convenience store (his hangout). He would carry on conversations with ease, often joking and showing a distinct sense of humor. However, Willie would become unusually quiet at school or around groups of strangers. Even his movements became more awkward and stiff.

Willie thought he could make it through high school. He said he knew an education was important for his future. Willie had expressed specific educational and occupational goals; he said he wanted to be a computer programmer. He also had an interest in general business, which he thought would help him in any job. He was looking forward to taking classes in computers and general business. Willie said that vocational-technical school was a viable opportunity for him. He was afraid that he could not go to college because he just didn't have the money. He said "we will just have to wait and see."

━━━

Willie's grandmother died last spring. He dropped out of school, but did complete his GED. He now has a full-time job with the newspaper and enjoys the privacy of a house he shares with his aunt.

LONNIE, CLASS CLOWN

"What's important in your life?" I asked Lonnie. "Finishing high school," he replied, and "going to college and playing sports." He laughed and said his family would kill him if he didn't finish high school, but he said he agreed with them. Although Lonnie said he was going to go to college he was unable to say specifically how he would accomplish his goal. He had little direct knowledge of how to go about it. He was a 15-year-old, African American tenth-grader living in a middle sized southern city. The largest employers were several universities and the municipal, county, and state governments. Like many teenagers he had lots of opinions and no hesitation in telling me about them. "I wish I could live in a big northern city. It's exciting! . . . Traveling on family vacations was great. . . . If I ever got a girl pregnant I might marry her, it depends. . . . I think Ted Bundy should have been executed for what he did. . . . I went to church every Sunday until I started working. . . . I know I'm smart and that I just need to do the work. . . . I think I'm doing a lot better now. I'm getting better grades."

Lonnie said he didn't have any particular problem. He didn't want to be singled out for any specific interventions or placed in any "special" programs. However, in stark contrast to his appearance and behavior, Lonnie's school record gave a different impression. Different teachers had different perceptions about Lonnie's nature and abilities and how Lonnie viewed himself. Lonnie's erratic grades indicated that he was capable of doing well academically, but something held him back. A documented history of teachers' comments should have been a red flag for intervention strategies, and yet apparently nothing much had been done. The interventions attempted within the last few years had failed. Despite their strengths, Lonnie's family had become confused, frustrated, and now felt powerless.

School Background

Lonnie entered the Head Start program at the age of three. The following year he attended a subsidized day care until starting kindergarten at age five. During 1978-79, Lonnie attended kindergarten in a northern state. He spent the first through the fourth grades in one school in his hometown, but he attended three different schools in fifth grade, when his family relocated to seek better employment. He attended summer school following fifth grade due to weak language, math, and reading skills and barely passed language arts. Throughout elementary school Lonnie was the subject of numerous parent-teacher conferences, primarily due to fighting. He also failed to complete work and had behavior problems.

He had not been retained or referred for testing. There was no record of formal interventions, evaluations, or retentions until the summer following fifth grade. Lonnie's mother noticed no vision or hearing difficulties, but records and teachers' comments indicated that testing might have been beneficial.

Lonnie attended two middle schools. He was in a middle-sized southern city for sixth and eighth grades, and in a large urban school in the North for seventh grade. Lonnie said that the seventh grade had been his favorite year in school. His records for sixth and eighth grades show multiple problems; he received frequent academic warnings during this time.

Sample teacher comments included the following: "must complete his folder; poor written work; incomplete assignments; does not follow directions; study habits unsatisfactory; poor attention; low test grades; missed test; lack of attention in class; failure to turn in homework; lack of interest; quality of work unsatisfactory; in-class work almost nonexistent; no improvement since last conference; low test scores; needs to make up tests; does not make up work missed; doesn't have a pencil; excessive talking; too talkative and disruptive; no passing grades so far." Despite such comments, no behavioral or academic warnings were recorded for sixth grade.

Lonnie attended summer school following eighth grade due to his failure to pass the school system's Instructional Management System Key Skills Test.

Lonnie attended ninth and tenth grade in the same southern city where he went to middle school. The high school, which has 1,700 students, is situated on a large expanse of land with facilities for a variety of sports. There are portable classrooms, and the one-story school has wings with wide covered walks between them. Each wing houses specific academic subjects.

The school population was about half male and half female; families' occupations were about one third professional, one third skilled, and one third semiskilled or unskilled. Nearly half the parents had advanced degrees, and about a third had twelve years of school or less. More than half the students (60%) had both parents living in the home. Students at this school, the third largest of four high schools, thought of the other schools in the area as "snob" schools. Their own teachers, they said, really cared about them. The students showed a lot of school spirit. Lonnie typified these attitudes. He said his mother tried to make him attend another school, but he said he liked most of his teachers and he had many friends at this school.

In the second semester of ninth grade, Lonnie was placed in Project Success, a program designed to be a bridge between middle school and high school for students considered at risk. Students in Project Success have a variety of problems, including, but not limited to low self-esteem, academic difficulties, family problems, poor coping skills, and the need for more individual attention. Lonnie attended all his classes with Project Success peers. He had the option of remaining in the program for tenth grade, but he opted out. His guidance counselor was disappointed. She thought the program might continue to help him. She met with Lonnie's mother several times and indicated that although Lonnie came from a loving and supportive home, it was unlikely that there would be home follow-through on school-based interventions. This realization by the counselor was the impetus for a conference she held with Lonnie, in which she stressed that he was responsible for his own behavior. To play sports and graduate he was told he would need to begin exerting his own control. Lonnie's behavior improved after the conference.

A Typical School Day

Lonnie awakened with difficulty at 6:30 a.m. His large closet was filled with designer clothes, and it took Lonnie extra time to decide what to wear each morning. After eating breakfast, Lonnie walked to a cousin's house where he caught a ride to school. School began at 7:27 a.m. with a class in intermediate construction (shop) in a portable classroom located behind the school. The class was fifty minutes long and students were free to work at their own pace and to talk with their classmates.

The shop teacher said Lonnie was strong-headed, intelligent, and basically a good kid. He acted as if he was an expert on everything but had trouble simply copying off the blackboard. One time he took an entire class period to write short assignments. According to the shop teacher Lonnie tended to play and was often not interested in working. He was immature. He tried to gain attention and used excuses when he failed to complete work. He avoided responsibility through tardiness and conflicts, but he was also a perfectionist. He threw away assignments because he thought they weren't good enough. He was a follower and had low self-esteem. He was uncomfortable with people, and occasionally acted up so that he would be allowed to work alone. Lonnie was the class clown. Although he could remain on task when motivated, he came to school to play.

The shop teacher thought Lonnie needed more follow-up at home. He discussed this issue with Lonnie's mother in a number of parent conferences. He believed Lonnie did as he pleased due to a lack of parental supervision. Lonnie was often on school grounds until 7:30 p.m.

If a student wants to learn, he will learn, said the shop teacher. Students who sought his help received it. Those who didn't were left alone. Lonnie's first semester grades in the shop teacher's class averaged a D.

After shop class, Lonnie walked to reading class, two portable buildings away. The room was neat and colorful, with traditional seating. The reading teacher's daily assignments reinforced basic reading skills. The teacher encouraged Lonnie to read aloud, but the large class size prevented him from doing this very often.

The reading teacher also said Lonnie had a self-esteem problem. Once he had become excessively sensitive when his basketball ability was questioned by another student. She said he was a follower and had been attracted to a bad crowd. Although she thought he was smart and had a good character, he was often tardy, frequently absent, and had trouble staying on task even though he wanted to do well. He was competitive and liked to argue. He wanted his own way much of the time and had natural leadership potential. However, he lacked self-discipline and did not want to be different from his classmates. He was talkative, defensive, did not accept responsibility when reprimanded, did not foresee consequences for misbehavior, and was immature. She thought he would probably graduate "just under the wire."

The reading teacher thought Lonnie needed more follow-through from his mother. Interventions agreed on at parent conferences were not carried out. When Lonnie was pushed to comply with school interventions and his mother's demands, he threatened to move out of state and live with his father. His mother feared that if he did he would drop out of high school.

The reading teacher admitted she found high school students difficult to deal with because her background was in elementary education. She had high expectations for her students' willingness to learn. She admitted that her interest in helping Lonnie had increased as his absenteeism had decreased. Lonnie had a D average for the first semester in the reading course.

At 9:20 a.m. Lonnie sauntered to his third-period world history class, nodding and gesturing to his friends and smiling freely. One friend reminded him not to forget baseball practice. On his way to fourth period, fundamental biology, Lonnie spoke briefly with a former girlfriend. He later told me they had broken up but they had had a brief rebound relationship.

Lonnie went to lunch just after 11:00 a.m. with his friend Herbert, who was also in the tenth grade. The two boys had been friends since the second grade, but due to work and school activities they saw each other less than they would have liked. Herbert said Lonnie was a loyal friend who would do anything for him. He also said that in the past they had ridden bicycles and played sports together, but now they mostly watched TV, played video games, went to the movies, and ate at fast-food restaurants. Sometimes they played pick-up basketball games or went to ball games. Herbert said they depended on an older friend with a car, so they often stayed at home. Both wanted to spend the next summer together in the northern city where Lonnie's father lived. They smiled as they spoke of the public transportation that would be available.

After lunch Lonnie went to English skills 2, which was taught by his favorite teacher. The classroom was crowded and had nearly blank walls. The desks were out of order. Lonnie sat next to the teacher so she could make sure he stayed on task. She explained that the other students would suffer if Lonnie received all the attention he desired.

Lonnie's English teacher said he was a late bloomer. He was very immature and everything was funny to him. She thought he had a good self-concept, but he was lazy and needed a great deal of attention. He did not seem to her to have any emotional hang-ups. He was not into drugs or alcohol. She thought he was intelligent, gregarious, impulsive, and artistic. One day, she thought, he would fulfill the family expectation of completing high school and going to college.

The English teacher had held several parent conferences with Lonnie's mother regarding Lonnie's lack of motivation. When she saw no improvement, she held a conference with all subject area teachers and Lonnie's mother. The group reached consensus, and the teacher compiled a goal sheet around specific teacher concerns. The goals included: arrive at school on time, stay on task, do not distract others, speak only with permission, follow instructions, stay in seat, stay out of gym after school, and have a good attitude. Lonnie's mother supported the goal sheet, but Lonnie thought it was childish and refused to follow it. The teacher felt frustrated that this intervention failed, but she continued to care about Lonnie and to modify her classroom methods to better satisfy his needs. He earned a C average for the semester in English skills 2.

Lonnie stayed after class chatting with friends and then had to rush to his first day of personal fitness class, which met in the gym. There were other classes in session in the gym and it was very noisy. The students sat on bleachers while the coach told them his requirements. He said they would need to keep a notebook in addition to participating in physical activities. The coach tried to stimulate discussion and Lonnie responded several times.

Earlier in the day Lonnie had told me the coach was his cousin. The coach later said he did not know Lonnie and was unaware that they were related, although he came from a large family and didn't know many of his cousins. He was unable to give me more information because he hadn't had Lonnie in a class before the current one.

At 1:32 p.m. Lonnie squeezed through the crowded walkways to his last class of the day, general math 2. The math teacher stood at the door, greeting students as they entered. There was much laughing and talking. It was a large class and all the seats were taken. The teacher wrote the previous day's assignments on the board and the students worked them out on the board during class. The teacher answered all questions during class to help those students having difficulty. The teacher said that for more advanced students like Lonnie the question period could be boring.

The math teacher said Lonnie had a poor self-concept and poor self-control. He did not stay on task and had a short attention span. "He's a puzzle," the teacher said, "an enigma. He should be in higher math but won't let himself do it. I never have to show him a problem more than once, and he is a nice kid. But he is also immature and would rather not buckle down to work." Although he had had poor attendance in the past, the teacher said he could see him getting into college and doing well.

The math teacher felt bad that he couldn't give Lonnie the extra attention he needed to advance to higher math. However, he also thought Lonnie would be uncomfortable in a higher math class because he would be leaving his friends behind. The teacher offered additional help to students after school. Lonnie had never taken advantage of that offer. He earned a C average for the semester in this class.

The school day ended at 2:27 p.m. Lonnie stayed on campus until baseball practice at 4:00 p.m. He said he looked forward to practice and was proud that his grades allowed him to play on a school team. The baseball coach said Lonnie was stubborn and didn't play as well as he could. The baseball coach echoed the other teachers as he told me Lonnie was immature and didn't try. He said he was a great athlete — a good pitcher and possibly even a great one — who was beginning to be noticed by other coaches. He said Lonnie could go to college if he got his act together in time.

After practice, Lonnie lingered on the school grounds shooting baskets before he began the 20-minute walk home.

Family Background

Lonnie lived with his maternal grandparents, his mother, and his 11-year-old sister in a three-bedroom house situated in a quiet, well-kept, low-income neighborhood. Inside, the house had a religious motif, although the family's activities seemed to center on the large-screen TV (equipped with video games) in the den.

Lonnie's mother worked part time for a large retail department store. She had a high school diploma and had attended two years of college. Her goal was to finish college and get more stable employment. Lonnie's grandmother had recently retired from the custodial staff of a large university in town. His grandfather was semi-retired from a maintenance position he had held for 20 years. The combined family income came from paid employment and social security benefits. Lonnie worked at a local fast-food restaurant for 16 hours each week.

Lonnie's mother and father were divorced. His father lived in a large northern city. He had a high school degree. Although he attended college, he dropped out to work full-time for the postal service, where he continued to work.

Lonnie's mother said her pregnancy was a positive experience. Lonnie weighed seven pounds, eleven ounces at birth and was a healthy child with no typical childhood diseases except for colic and a brief time in a corrective shoe brace. He spoke in sentences at ten months. At age four, Lonnie had a severe adjustment problem when his younger sister was born. He acted up often and had frequent stomachaches. At age six, he was struck by a drunk driver while bicycle riding with a friend. He suffered no permanent injuries. Lonnie received regular health care throughout his childhood. A psychologist evaluated Lonnie for possible hyperactivity at age seven, but results from the observation indicated no reason to pursue further testing.

Lonnie's mother said he was very close to his grandmother, probably because she had been his primary caregiver for much of his early childhood. Lonnie's mother would like to have shared a closer relationship with him, but she felt unable to do so. Lonnie, however, said he was closest to his mother.

Despite some sibling rivalry, Lonnie eventually developed a normal relationship with his sister. Lonnie's grandfather administered discipline when motherly attempts failed. Lonnie's father remained a central figure in his life, even though he had not been in the home since the parent's divorce 11 years ago. Lonnie spent most of his summers with his father, and talked to him on the telephone every week. Lonnie's mother reported that Lonnie idolized his father and was defensive about him. She was unable to criticize Lonnie's father in his presence. The father didn't supplement the family income through child support, although he occasionally sent Lonnie gifts and money.

Lonnie's mother described her divorce as "ugly." Following a legal battle, Lonnie's father was awarded custody and from age four and a half to age six Lonnie had remained with him. At the end of that time Lonnie's mother received custody. According to his mother, when Lonnie returned to her he had undergone a personality change. He had changed from a quiet child to a "monster." He was overactive, demanding, and refused to obey his mother. Gradually, however, these behaviors subsided.

Lonnie's mother said she was dissatisfied with her current life situation. She indicated that her life had not gone as she envisioned it would. She didn't like being financially dependent on her elderly parents and responsible for their care. She didn't want to live in her present community. While she didn't regret her divorce, she regretted the frequent moves and disruptions it had caused. Two attempts at reconciliation with her husband had resulted in incidents of spouse abuse. She said that to her knowledge Lonnie's father had never abused him.

Lonnie's mother described Lonnie as very smart, stubborn, secretive, and active. She was proud of him but very distressed about his school problems. She believed he was responsible for these difficulties but believed that he would eventually outgrow them. According to her, Lonnie was modeling his father's attitudes about school rather than the values she had tried to instill in him. She thought she would always need to counteract the influence of Lonnie's father. Despite her current life situation, Lonnie's mother was optimistic about the future.

Suggested Interventions

In his booklet *High School Dropouts: Causes, Consequences and Cures*, Donald R. Grossnickle suggested that the following signs can give early warning of students at risk: poor attendance, tardiness, consistently low grades, lack of basic skills (especially reading), home problems, poor communication between home and school, history of school transfers and family moves, failure to see the relevance of education, older sibling or parent being a drop-out, and low self-esteem.

Lonnie displayed many of these signs, including tardiness, consistently poor grades, and frequent moves. However, there were mitigating influences: Lonnie's immediate family was supportive and his extended family stable; there was frequent communication between mother and school; he had no apparent drug use; both parents had graduated from high school; and Lonnie had never been retained.

Some school people said Lonnie had low self-esteem, while some said his self-esteem was high. On the Rosenberg Self-Esteem Scale Lonnie scored 33 of a possible 40 points, indicating an above-average sense of self.

Intervention strategies to reinforce Lonnie's recent improvement could include: increasing positive incentives; intervening with school personnel in order to enhance their perception of Lonnie; including Lonnie in the development of any future interventions; encouraging Lonnie to accept after-school instruction to enhance his natural math abilities; advocating for additional individualized baseball instruction; encouraging parent participation in Lonnie's activities; assisting Lonnie's mother as needed with employment and education; enhancing the positive relationship between Lonnie and his favorite teacher.

Lonnie is presently a senior (1991), attending the same high school and living at the same address. School personnel, including the guidance counselor, assistant principal for student affairs, and two teachers said Lonnie is a success story. He is currently enrolled in the Cooperative Business Education program (CBE), which is available for second semester seniors. He reports to a first period English class each day and then works at his uncle's concrete company for the rest of the day. He has shown good work initiative and has received As in the program. Reports from the school indicate the following:

> Lonnie has had no discipline referrals this year. He was able to play on the varsity basketball team for most of the season. He is presently running track.
>
> Lonnie has gained in self-confidence and popularity.
>
> Lonnie is described as a model kid, one who has gotten it together.
>
> Lonnie's future plans are to attend a junior college in New York near to his father's home.

Lonnie is proud of his successes but stated, "I know I can do better." He is anxious to finish high school and gain some independence. He plans to enlist in the Air Force Reserves this summer to obtain income for his college tuition.

MIKE, SMALL-TOWN BOY

Mike at School

The day Mike and I met, his shirttail hung out of his jeans and his neatly trimmed brown hair fell midway down his neck. He spoke softly as we talked about school activities, and when academics were mentioned he appeared to tense slightly, moving his hands in concert with his now somewhat strained voice. He was a congenial young man, heavyset and just under six feet tall.

Mike said his small community elementary school (K-5) was the best of the five schools he had attended. His teachers were nice, he had fun, and he made good grades, a report confirmed by his cumulative records. In the third grade he received Es (excellent) or Gs (good) despite his excessive absences related to asthma and bronchitis. Through the seventh grade Mike continued to receive As and Bs, and he had much better attendance.

Standardized achievement test scores for seventh-grade work were above average in mathematics and reading. A Slosson Intelligence Test administered in fifth grade revealed an I.Q. of 127. There was no suggestion in any record that he functioned below grade level in any curriculum area.

It was only in grades 8 and 9 that Cs, Ds, and Fs started to creep into Mike's academic record. However, even then standardized test scores continued to indicate that he was at or above grade level in achievement.

Mike's home state requires statewide testing of minimum basic skills competency in grades 3, 5, 8, and 10 in the areas of math and communications (reading and writing). The results of these periodic tests revealed that Mike had few, if any, problems.

Grade 3　　All math and communications standards were mastered.

Grade 5　　All math standards except one were mastered (graphs); all communications standards except one were mastered (main idea).

Grade 8   All math standards except one were mastered (division using decimals); all communications standards were mastered.

Grade 10   All math standards except one were mastered (division using decimals); all communications standards were mastered. The literacy test was passed.

Last summer Mike went to summer school to retake science and math. He passed, with a C and B respectively. His science teacher noted that his behavior was poor and that he didn't apply himself.

At the time of our interview his record for this year showed that first semester he had passed only two classes, both in Peer Counseling I, a class that involved work with exceptional-education students in a special school nearby. He had heard about the class in an announcement over the school speaker one day. Interested students were invited, schedules permitting, to sign up to work at the school. He was accepted, and for the third and fourth periods each day he assisted severely retarded and handicapped students with assignments for six weeks. The assignments included speech, gardening (for some, this was learning how to water plants), and crafts (which were sold at the school's country store each Christmas). Mike said he liked to work with these students. As we continued to talk, he mentioned that he had missed 38 days of school.

Mike thought that the attitude of some of his teachers could have improved. Whenever he did some little thing they considered bad, they "got on his case" and wouldn't get off. Mike complained that one of his teachers conducted his science class like a college class. He said the amount of paperwork in the class was unbelievable, and there were too many chapter tests. Other teachers skipped around in the text, which created problems for him. If he was absent for a day or two and tried to keep up at home by doing the next chapter, it never worked, because they often didn't do the next chapter.

His favorite class was history, which he failed first semester, while the class he liked least was English, which he also failed first semester and, ultimately, for the year. During his junior high school years his most enjoyable class was agriculture.

He thought the high school atmosphere, including the incentive to do better, would improve if one period was cut from the seven-period day. The day would thus end a little earlier, and he would have more time for studies, work, or doing other things he liked to do.

Mike favored electronics as a career. Though he had no plans to go to college, he said he would like to take a course in automotive body work at one of the district's vocational schools so that he would be able to take care of his own car. When I discussed a problem I was having with an oil leak in my car and mentioned the special hose my mechanic had ordered, he immediately told me that could not be the problem unless the oil was a certain color. He was correct.

When asked what he thought could be part of the problem with his work at school, he admitted that he needed to help himself more. He had made up his mind that he wanted to graduate from high school. Even though he knew that he'd have to go to summer school as he did last summer and that he'd enter the next school year minus some credits, he was going to stay with it. Mike said that he was trying to pick up his studies this semester by trying harder and attending classes regularly.

There was no evidence that Mike used drugs or alcohol or that he was sexually active; he never mentioned girls during the interview. I found two suspension notices in his file. In eighth grade he was suspended from riding the bus for three days for using tobacco and spitting on the bus; while in ninth grade he was suspended from school six days for fighting on school property.

Mike's math teacher had had him as a student for only one six-week period (second semester). The teacher who had previously taught remedial math with an enrollment of 18 students now had Mike's basic math class with 30 students, many of whom were learning disabled students participating in a special exceptional education program. None of the students in the class, including Mike, showed any interest in math. Their attitude was that there was no real necessity for learning any of that. Although the teacher thought that a practical, hands-on approach would be more appropriate, he did not indicate that he thought such an approach could be implemented in the present setting.

The math teacher said he used direct instruction and then moved about the room giving individual assistance as needed. He did not group the students, because he felt he could not maintain control and productivity from these non-motivated students.

He further commented that many of the students in this class appeared to be from low-income families.

Mike was passing the course with either a "low C or a high D." He had one examination yet to take, which the teacher thought he would pass. Mike did just enough work to get by. If the assignment took approximately 30 minutes, he finished in 15, with most of the answers correct but with few calculations showing. He didn't want to take the time to write them all down. When he finished early, he often made noises that distracted the other students.

Finally Mike was sent to a guidance counselor because of his behavior. His seat was moved to the front of the room, and the teacher noted that Mike was on work detail in the afternoons after school. Because Mike rode the bus, his grandmother had to drive 10 miles each way to pick him up when he finished his detail.

Mike at Home

Mike's grandmother was quite willing to talk over the telephone, but she did not welcome a home visit by anyone who wanted to gather information. At the outset she said that she did not have much formal education but that she thought education was important and that she wanted her grandson to stay in school and get his diploma. She had found the working world hard without a diploma, and she didn't want Mike to have the same experience.

Abandoned by his mother at the age of three weeks, Mike was raised by his grandparents. His father lived in a trailer on the grandparents' property, but according to the grandmother, he had little to say about Mike. The father was the grandparents' son and Mike was the only grandchild. The only other reference Mike's grandmother made to her son was that he wanted Mike to drop out of school at age 16 — since he was having problems with grades — and then start back again the next year. She objected to this strenuously. Once Mike quit she knew very well that he would never go back to school.

Mike was raised in a small community where the grandparents at one time had owned a small citrus company. The grandmother told how Mike had enjoyed working with his grandfather in their garden. Long before he went to school he had learned to read the names of vegetables from the seed packages. She thought he seemed really bright. He also had enjoyed going to the citrus groves with his grandfather as well as fishing in the many lakes not far from their home. When Mike was 10, his grandfather died. He never spoke of this, or of anything else about which he feels deeply, according to his grandmother. "He's quiet; he just won't tell you how he feels." During those years he had no neighbors, so he spent most of his time out of school riding his bike and watching television.

Although standard English is the language of the home, it was enriched with his grandmother's southern colloquialisms. She did not work outside the home; however, she had worked briefly in a school cafeteria. Mike's father worked in an automotive shop.

Nursery school was not a part of Mike's early education; however, he did attend kindergarten. He was not retained in any grade, although he did have to attend summer school at the end of ninth grade because he had failed two subjects. When asked if any part of her grandson's education had been particularly effective, Mike's grandmother could think of none. Nor did she have any suggestions for content or strategies that might have prevented some of Mike's academic problems. She basically accepted what the schools were doing and placed the blame primarily on her grandson for any difficulty Mike might have had.

Mike had attended the K-5 elementary school in the small community where he lived. His grandmother recalled no particular problems during that time. The middle school (sixth grade), two junior highs (one for seventh grade, and one for eighth and ninth grade), and the senior high school he attended were in a town about 10 miles away. It was at the second junior high school that she believed school problems had begun.

Mike told his grandmother at that time and continued to tell her that his teachers picked on him; that they were real hard on him and didn't like him. While she believed this could happen if there was a student-teacher conflict, she doubted it was true in this case. Mike didn't bring any work home and shrugged off questions about school. She thought he didn't study as hard he should and discovered from his most recent school that he didn't turn in assignments.

On one occasion, after being contacted by the school, she realized that he hadn't brought home letters or notes sent from the school. She talked sternly to him about this and his lack of productiveness at school. She thought she had to talk to him, that she could not "beat" on him.

In junior high school agriculture seemed to have been his favorite subject. She mentioned his fondness for the teacher (an experienced professional) and that one year he had raised a lamb as a project. All of the family enjoyed the lamb, but once it was sold, Mike wouldn't raise another animal of any kind.

During two telephone conversations Mike's grandmother spoke forcefully about youngsters today and their lack of responsibility. She went on to say that all Mike was interested in was music and cars. To further emphasize her point, she told how earlier she had given her grandson her "little" truck, which he managed to wreck in a short time. She then bought him an old car, which he and two friends abandoned by the side of the road one evening, when it developed mechanical problems. Someone smashed the car's windows, and Mike tried to get her to buy him a new one. She refused, emphasizing that he had to understand why she wouldn't. "He ain't grown," she concluded, "and he's trying to get over 'fool's mountain.' "

She thought Mike's ambition was to work on small motors or to do bodywork on cars, like his dad. She said he wanted to take the small-motor training at one of the district's vocational schools.

Throughout our phone conversations, Mike's grandmother continued to emphasize the importance of an education and how not having one had made her life more difficult. She spoke as a determined person; she did not mince words. She showed no reticence when addressing a problem, nor did she blame Mike's problems on others. She spoke plainly, with little expression, except when addressing today's youth and their irresponsibility.

According to his grandmother, Mike did not think his clothes were as good as the clothes his peers wore. She said, however, "They're clean and he should be happy to have them." And she further admonished him that he had a home to come to and for that he should be grateful.

Mike said he had an old car that he tried to keep running since he and his friends liked to cruise to some of the larger neighboring towns to see what was going on. He also enjoyed playing basketball with his friends, either on the courts at the elementary school or at one of their homes. He said he had quite a few friends and that he got along fine with them.

Mike did not buy his present car; his dad had bought it for him. He did not work during the school year, however, he had worked with a crew the previous summer picking up citrus limbs that had been trimmed from the trees. He said it was really hot work, and he hoped to work in his uncle's auto repair shop after the summer school session was over (he was sure he would have to attend).

Postscript

A new school year began amid the intense heat of late August. Mike did not enroll. The records indicated that Mike had not even enrolled in summer school. He was not enrolled in the adult school for the area nor in either of the two vocational schools in the district. No school had requested his records.

"The last time we talked, toward the end of the school year, he felt sad about his school situation, even though he had a grade point average of 1.8," his occupational guidance specialist observed. "We talked for a long while, and when he left to go I thought that he felt encouraged, that once again he was looking toward a future in the automotive field."

His student record listed two phone numbers. Recordings for both dutifully noted that they were no longer in service. Sadly, I concluded that Mike had become a drop-out. Many questions remain unanswered:

- What happened to that significant other, the grandmother, and her influence of determination and hope for her grandson?

- What happened during the summer that not even automotive training at a vocational center could entice Mike to return for another year? Was it a full-time job? A new car? Peer pressure? A serious personal problem?

Perhaps there was something prophetic for Mike, as well as for many of today's students, in the parting words of the occupational specialist: "I've seen lots of students enter high school with fairly good grades, with graduation as their goal, and then gradually they have to let something slip when they begin to work 30 to 35 hours a week to support the car habit. Usually it's the academics, and then it's school itself."

No further information about Mike is available. His grand-mother moved and there is no forwarding address.

CRYSTAL, A GIFTED DROPOUT

WHY?

Why don't people understand
The way I am?
Why don't people ever show
That I am known?
Why?
Why don't people seem to care
When I am there?
Why doesn't anyone yearn to be
More like me?
Why?
Why don't people even try
To say hi
When I walk by?
Why do people turn away
When I stray?
Why?
Why are all people like you?
I haven't a clue.
I am not like you.
Why?

Crystal, 1986

Crystal was gifted, but very much at risk. Although a student of high ability and many talents, she dropped out of school and began learning at home through the district's correspondence school.

I first met Crystal five years ago, when she quietly entered my gifted classroom. I thought she was shy. Her academic and emotional behaviors were typical of her classmates. She was tall and slightly overweight. Her skin was fair, her hair was strawberry blonde, and her eyes were oval. Through the years, she experimented with different hair and dress styles — one summer she dyed her hair midnight black and got a mohawk. The rest of her appearance was conservative and typical of today's styles.

Elementary teachers and school personnel remembered her as quiet, average in appearance, and overweight. Four of the five elementary people interviewed said Crystal was pushed to perform in talent shows and to participate in tap and ballet lessons. They thought she was self-conscious because she was overweight, and wearing a tutu did not flatter her figure. Since she seldom spoke in class or volunteered information, they thought performing was probably very difficult for her.

Crystal's perception of herself can best be found by looking at her creative writing and her music. Since early elementary school her interests had been music and literature. Locally, she won many writing contests, and one summer, with a friend, she won first place at the state fair for a singing arrangement. Many of her writings reflect her ability to see unique relationships and reflect her view of the world. Her seventh-grade English teacher stated she was a very good creative writer.

The writings turned in to me reflected themes of self-exploration and were very perceptive. It was not easy for Crystal to share her writings, since they were very personal. She once told her elementary teacher she didn't want her mother to know when she had done something exceptionally well, because her mother would embarrass her by bragging about it.

Crystal's mom described her as highly gifted and musically talented, but painfully shy until junior high school. In her first year of preschool Crystal did not talk until April.

While in the third grade, she got a recorder and her mother said she was the music leader of her class. In the fourth grade she began to learn the saxophone. Her parents said, each at separate interviews, that Crystal cried the first night she got her saxophone because she could not make it "sound good."

When Crystal chose to do something her commitment to the task was phenomenal. When she broke her hand, she convinced the doctor not to put on a cast so that she could play in the concert that week. She learned to write with her other hand so she could do all her homework, even though she was excused from much of the work.

Crystal was very sensitive and saw things from many different viewpoints. Almost all the people interviewed said she was quiet and always considerate of others' feelings. She was quick to defend anyone who might be mistreated or misunderstood. When asked what she'd like to be, she said, "Black, they have more fun. I like their music and they are considerate of other people." One reason Crystal said she dropped out of school was, "It's the people, they're just so immature. They don't like anyone who is different."

Crystal had high expectations of herself and others. However, her parents suggested her expectations were too high. In 1988, when Crystal was having difficulties at high school, her mom convinced her to talk to me. After several hours of discussion, we agreed she would spend a day talking to a variety of people in different educational settings to see what options existed for her. I asked her to list the rights she had as a student and write a personal contract she would like to follow. The contract consisted of the goals she had for schools she'd like to attend and the steps she had to take to accomplish these goals were reached. Crystal said, "I'm planning to live up to everyone's expectations of me, including my own." Although she noted that a good attitude and her family's support as resources needed to reach her goals, she stated that laziness, self-doubt, and self-criticism were the real roadblocks to her reaching her goals.

Her mother suggested that Crystal didn't understand her talents. She played music by ear and, until recently, was not aware that others could not. When her brother asked her to transpose a song from the radio, she couldn't understand why he couldn't do it himself.

At the age of four Crystal started dancing. Throughout elementary school she was in tap dance and music lessons. Her elementary teachers seemed to think she was pushed to perform, but Crystal was never afraid to sing, dance, or play her musical instrument on stage. She knew her musical ability was good, and she was not afraid to tell people she was good or to share her talent.

In many ways Crystal was a very confident and intelligent child willing to work hard for what she wanted. If she promised something, she would persevere and do whatever she had promised. She said that somehow she was going to pursue a musical career, but later she became confused and wondered which way to go. Crystal wrote many poems, including the following, that reflected her needs and feelings:

> At times I wonder just what my life
> Would be like
> If I knew who I was made of.
> I'm almost afraid to find out
> Now that I am old enough to
> Face the consequences.
> But I don't really know if it would have
> Mattered to me
> As a child. . . .
> It's all very confusing to me at times.
> Like now.
> So I'm always wondering
> Never knowing.
>
> *Crystal, 1988*

At Home

The family lived in a run-down three-story house within walking distance of Crystal's elementary school. The principal of the school said her parents moved to this house to be in the school's attendance area. Mom wanted a multicultural school that was small enough for her children to receive individual attention.

The house was full of memorabilia and pictures that gave it a homey atmosphere. The family had a dog, snakes, hamster, parakeet, and a large, elaborate aquarium.

The Family

Crystal was nine weeks old when she was adopted. She was the second in the family of five adopted children. When Crystal was in fifth grade the family adopted a Korean baby girl they named Hannah. In Crystal's eighth-grade year they adopted a dwarf Korean boy named David, who had been malnourished and abused. The family planned to adopt another dwarf child because the mother thought David would adjust better with another dwarf in the family. Crystal had a different relationship with each of her siblings.

Brad, age 19, was the oldest and an identified gifted child. He quit high school and now works at a fast-food restaurant. When she was in eighth grade, Crystal thought Brad's dress, appearance, and behavior were bizarre and unacceptable. She did not understand his lack of achievement in school performance. Brad was known as a waver (local slang for drug user) and his involvement with drugs was confirmed. Crystal and Brad never communicated well. As they got older the communication seemed to break down to the point of complete separation. Crystal resented Brad's behavior and attitudes because of the impact they had on the family. Her mother said Crystal considered herself physically abused by Brad, but saw this as typical sibling rivalry. The family tried professional joint counseling to ease this situation, but the mother thought it had been ineffective.

Curt, age 11, had a very close relationship with Crystal. He was outgoing and verbal, and because she was shy, Crystal often asked Curt to speak for her. She was willing to help Curt with his homework and at times would do it for him. She wanted him to be successful.

Hannah, age 6, was the peacemaker of the family. The mother described her as loving everyone. She went to the mother whenever she thought one of the children was being mean. The mother said Hannah's relationship with Crystal was perhaps the best relationship of all the siblings.

David, age 5, was a very loud child. He recognized that his mother had the first authority, then Crystal. For the first year after his adoption, Crystal was the only person who could put David to sleep. Her mother described Crystal's relationship as a love-hate relationship. At times Crystal was extremely loving and caring and at other times completely out of bounds with him, threatening to send him back to Korea or to cut off his sixth toe.

Both father and mother mentioned that Crystal had resented the adoption of David. She asked her mother why they had to take in misfits and why they had to adopt all these kids. Her

95

mother thought that Crystal felt if the family wasn't so large, her mother could focus more on her.

Crystal and her father did not spend much time together. His job required him to be away from home for long periods of time. When he was home his time was spent with the family as a whole. He said, "Crystal and I, one on one, have never been much." He thought Crystal was uncomfortable with him. According to her mother, Crystal never cared for the males who were related to her.

Crystal's adopted mother was the prime nurturer of the family. She said that until seventh grade Crystal had been dependent on her. The mother did not work, but was an enthusiastic volunteer; she called herself a professional volunteer; she was very active in the schools, Boy Scouts and Girl Scouts, and other community organizations. But she was also interested in all aspects of her adopted children's lives. Crystal often babysat when her mother attended meetings or other activities. They paid her for babysitting, not as much as a normal babysitter, but it was her primary household chore. A couple of teachers in the middle school thought she spent too much time caring for the other children.

Her mother described Crystal as perceptive and intelligent. "When Crystal was two and a half years old," she said, "we were sitting around the table discussing the adoption of Curt. We've always openly discussed adoption and who and why we were adopting. Brad said he was born in the hospital. Crystal asked where she was born. When she was told that she had been born in a cabin in the woods, Crystal said. 'oh, yes, I remember the woods were dark and tangled.' "

Her mother thought her relationship with Crystal was very close, but she also questioned her own parenting skills. Crystal was rebelling, and her mother said "she feels caged, inhibited by the family and me."

It was important for Crystal to search for her birth mother. Her adoptive mother also wanted to know who Crystal's birth mother was and what she was like. She thought this information might help them both to better understand each other. She resented that Crystal did not consider her to be her mother. The mother said Crystal was not considerate of her feelings and did not appreciate her. She said Crystal often pushed the limits and she was afraid one day Crystal would just disappear.

Crystal said when she finally got to leave, she would never look back. She couldn't understand why Brad, who left home, called home and recently had come home for a visit.

Crystal's mother and father seemed to have a very stable relationship. Her mother made most of the decisions about the children because she was there all the time. With the father gone every other week, it was sometimes difficult for him to be involved in conferences and other school activities.

School personnel did not know the father well, but they said if asked, that he was available for help or input.

Crystal's Friends

Crystal had high ideals for herself and others. According to her mother, Crystal's friendships were deep and long lasting; she was very faithful to and defensive of her friends. She seemed to have understanding beyond her years. Her mother said she was not a people pleaser and she could be bossy and opinionated, but that she did try to be considerate. Her elementary teachers said she had a very good sense of right and wrong, but her mother said Crystal's sense of right and wrong was different from other people's.

Her mother was concerned about her friends. "She is only 15 and when she goes to the local amusement center she meets GIs." She was once grounded because two GIs came by the house and helped her crawl out her bedroom window. She and the two GIs were picked up in a parking lot at 1:00 a.m. Her parents had to pick up Crystal at the police station. Crystal couldn't see what she had done wrong, "all we were doing was talking."

Crystal's friends in elementary school were involved in Scouting and music. They were stable individuals and longtime friends. When interviewing the high school counselor, I met a student who had been Crystal's friend throughout elementary and middle school. She spoke very highly of Crystal and said she and Crystal had competed throughout eighth grade. Though they were very close, she couldn't figure out why they had drifted apart. She thought Crystal had dropped out of school because the teachers didn't understand her. She wished Crystal and she were still friends because she really missed her.

Crystal was exuberant in middle school; it was probably her happiest time. Teachers recalled that she had several groups of friends and got along well with her peers. She particularly enjoyed her friends in the gifted and talented class. Most of them were very motivated and she could work on many projects with different groups of people. Crystal did not have a particular boyfriend, but she related well to several boys and openly chased one relentlessly. Yet, Crystal could also be very insecure and lacked trust in males.

High school was different. Crystal saw high school students as immature, not concerned about others or their ideas, too involved with what to wear and who was going with whom, and categorizing people. She said the friendships these people formed were superficial, "they just don't mean anything."

Her mother said Crystal tended to form addictive relationships. She always had many acquaintances, but usually was close with only one person at a time. This friend could easily persuade her to do anything, even shoplift. Her mother seemed to think part of Crystal's troubles were related to the type of friends she had developed.

Crystal's mother was worried. Two of her children had dropped out of school and she feared a pattern was forming. She thought the teachers would have the same expectations for her other children and that Brad would be the model the other children would follow. Crystal resented the fact that school personnel compared her with Brad. He had had trouble in high school and they assumed his sister would also, she said.

School

School people had different perceptions of Crystal. All those I interviewed said she had tremendous written language ability and was a great creative writer. They often mentioned her musical ability.

Although Crystal was in the gifted and talented program, elementary teachers did not view her as exceptionally gifted; she did not always work to her full potential and was an underachiever in some classes. They thought she was an overachiever who was pushed hard to succeed. They said that Crystal's mother was too involved in her educational program.

High school teachers declined to be interviewed because they didn't think they knew Crystal well enough. Only the high school counselor agreed to be interviewed. She believed Crystal was extremely gifted and perhaps should have gone straight to the university from eighth grade. She said Crystal's mother always attended staff meetings and was very concerned about her daughter. She also believed Crystal did poorly due to attendance problems and her unwillingness to do what was required of her. She considered her a very gifted individual who didn't fit into the high school program.

Other school people saw Crystal as a quiet girl with high expectations, but did not see her as a leader in any way. The principal of her elementary school did mention that although Crystal was not a verbal leader, she had once accompanied a group of students that came to his office with a number of demands.

Ninth Grade

In the spring of Crystal's ninth-grade year she ran away from home. She and a friend took a cab to a neighboring town. Crystal's mother picked them up and paid the cab fare. She didn't punish Crystal in any way. She thought Crystal only did this because the girl she ran away with was being abused at home. Her mother thought Crystal went along just to help the other girl, but she was concerned that she might do it again "just to make a break" — and that she wouldn't come back. She implied this was a good learning experience for Crystal. The police and social service agencies saw it as a lark.

Incidents like these and failing grades led Crystal's parents to believe that drugs were causing the trouble. Perhaps because Brad had been involved in drugs, they feared Crystal would as well. Her mother began to see Crystal's running away and other rebellious actions as symptoms of something else that might have been wrong. Her parents took Crystal to a local drug and alcohol assessment center, which reported Crystal was not involved in drugs or alcohol, not sexually active, and didn't have any problems they could see. Subsequently, Crystal's mother took her to a treatment program to see if they could provide counseling for Crystal. The program wanted to do a three-week neurological assessment before counseling her, after which Crystal would have to be in the program for a prolonged period. Since no neurological problems had ever been indicated, and Crystal was apparently not involved with drugs or alcohol, her mother was unsure that the expensive program would help. As Crystal continued to repeat a favorite phrase "Right now, who cares?" her mother worried that Crystal would marry since she was vulnerable and might see marriage as an escape.

According to her mother, it was hard to believe Crystal was only 15. She spoke and acted much older. Her mother said she just wanted her to be happy and to have self-confidence. She didn't care what lifestyle Crystal chose or what sexual preference she had if she was happy. She said Crystal had no focus in life except Friday night and her one friend. Her mother thought Crystal would be very susceptible to joining a cult because she was vulnerable to suggestion and because she was involved in organized religion and "eating it all up." Although the father was agnostic, Crystal's mother described herself as very spiritual.

Over the years, Crystal's teachers have had very different opinions about her. A gifted-talented elementary teacher said, "Crystal will never be successful in a traditional school program. She needs to get away from her family." Another elementary teacher said, "I see Crystal as being very successful in school." Her middle school counselor said, "Perhaps she would be better off in a performing arts school or in a mentor relationship." A middle school teacher said, "Ultimately, I think Crystal will be okay if she gets some help to sort through her needs and concerns. What would be best would be for her to find a mentor. Crystal does best when she personally makes a commitment." And a high school counselor said, "I don't think Crystal will be successful because she has blown it and she doesn't and won't get the training she needs."

Crystal and Her Parents' View of the School Program

To some extent, school worked well for Crystal until the ninth grade. But there were hints of future problems earlier than that. Crystal couldn't or wouldn't say what happened, or why she did not remain in the conventional high school. When questioned she said, "It's the people, they are just so immature." When asked if it was the teachers, she said they simply weren't that bad. When asked if it was the curriculum, she said, "It's OK, but it's just so boring. Why do we have to learn all that stuff? It doesn't make any sense. The school here just wasn't for me. The correspondence courses are easy and I can do them at my own pace." She didn't understand why certain requirements were so rigid; she wanted credit for her own creative projects.

After dropping out of high school and enrolling in the correspondence school, she finished a year and a half of credits in six months. She hoped to finish all her high school requirements by her sixteenth or seventeenth birthday.

Crystal's parents did not exactly understand what had happened, but they had a few ideas why Crystal did not make it in the regular school setting. Her father thought her personality traits conflicted with any institutional setting. She had an aversion to fitting in with the masses and did not want to be part of a group. He said she had always been that way, even to the point of rebellion. He said if you opened her up, you would see a very bright, talented, and volatile individual.

The correspondence school filled a need, but he wanted her involvement in education to be more consistent. She wasn't forming the right habits or challenging herself. He wanted her to go back into the regular school setting, but didn't think that would happen.

Crystal's father thought school should be done differently. Both his oldest children rebelled against rote learning. He said every year the students started over and did basics before they got to the new stuff. That often led to boredom. There were no alternatives at the high school level, and Crystal did not want to attend the alternative high school because she thought most of the kids there were "druggies and really weird."

Crystal's mother said there was something wrong with a system that couldn't help gifted children. She said there should be flexible programs for students who don't fit in and suggested this could be done by having a school for the gifted. She also said school shouldn't make students take courses they hate. School would have been easier for Crystal, her mother said, if she had not been gifted. She thought Crystal had done well in elementary school and middle school because people cared for her there. Teachers at the high school care, she said, but they do not understand gifted students. They are so busy getting students up to norm they can't keep gifted children challenged. She suggested that when children get to high school they are ready for more than book learning. They need physical and technical skills. None of her children liked the extracurricular program. It just didn't offer them any challenges. The mother would like to see the school system better organized so children like Crystal could be successful.

Testing

Crystal took the Slosson Intelligence Test twice (at age five years, one month and at age seven years, seven months). On both occasions she scored in the superior range.

In 1984 the Structure of the Intellect (SOI) testing for the gifted-talented program showed her strengths to be math, language comprehension, short and long-term memory, form reasoning, logic and verbal fluency, and creativity. Her relative weaknesses were reasoning with words, figural closure, and convergent recognition of symbols.

Individual gifted-talented tests confirmed she could be an exceptional academic student in all areas. It was significant to note that Crystal's early achievement in math fell off drastically as she progressed through the school system. Her mother blamed the school for Crystal losing her self-confidence in math.

Achievement testing also showed Crystal's ability in the written language area. Her reading remained consistently exceptional through the years. Her relative weakness, knowledge (social science and science area), dropped as she progressed through the system.

The scores of the standardized tests given outside the gifted-talented program were consistent with the gifted-talented testing. Spelling and social studies were consistently her weakest areas. Language arts remained her strongest area. Math was a very strong achievement area until the onset of adolescence.

Report Cards and Attendance

Until she entered high school, Crystal's grades were As and Bs, and her attendance was good. When Crystal dropped out of high school and enrolled in the correspondence school, she was failing all classes except elementary algebra, in which she had a D-. Her attendance was poor. According to the high school counselor, Crystal said her attendance was poor because she was sick, didn't like what was happening in class, and just couldn't go to class. Her mother said she wouldn't get out of bed unless coerced. No one could explain why Crystal did not want to go to school.

Comments on Crystal's report cards from kindergarten through eighth grade usually included the following phrases: student is a pleasure to have in class; work is outstanding; effort is excellent and enthusiastic. Very few negative comments were noted on any report card from kindergarten through the eighth grade. A couple of quarterly comments in middle school indicated that homework needed to be done. All comments noted after eighth grade were negative, except to say the student was a pleasure to have in class: missing assignments; make-up work not in; student is not working up to potential; low test scores; excessive absences are slowing progress. The counselor at the high school thought Crystal was "living in the sixties": just rebelling because it was the thing to do. When asked if gifted students or high achievers often had trouble in high school, the counselor said, "We lose a lot more than we admit to. When you get to high school the students really don't have a lot of choices. They have a lot of required courses they have to take and many of the students don't understand that."

Regular Education Program

Other than the gifted-talented program, Crystal had no modification of curriculum. Her mother thought the lack of special attention led to Crystal's withdrawal from school. The gifted program was what had kept Crystal going and when that was withdrawn at high school with nothing to replace it, Crystal stopped functioning. Crystal demanded a purpose for knowing something. We discussed enrollment in a university music methods class. It was a very difficult class, but Crystal was willing to put the time in to help improve her music writing. Her mother thought Crystal was a liberated female; she said Crystal knew what she wanted.

Gifted and Talented Program

Crystal was referred to and qualified for the gifted-talented program in kindergarten. The services at the elementary level were primarily enrichment. On the reevaluation parent referrals, her mother made the following comments: "Crystal was a very capable, serious person; she takes life, especially school, very seriously; she often pressures herself too much."

Crystal made the following comments on her evaluation forms: "I like to color; I like the things we do and it is really fun to do things that I know how to do; this class is a special class and I like it; I feel good in this room with this nice teacher; I like G/T because there is always something to do."

In middle school gifted-talented classes were scheduled so that students were not pulled from other classes. Crystal took gifted-talented for an elective in seventh grade and advanced reading literature. In the eighth grade Crystal had two of her seven classes in the gifted-talented room. Because of her exceptionally high scores in written language, she did not take regular English. Yet, she worked on special English projects with the gifted-talented teacher. Crystal also took an advanced social studies class. Although social studies was very difficult for her, she wanted to be with the gifted-talented students. Her middle school gifted-talented teacher indicated Crystal did very well in social science if she could personalize her projects. The teacher referred to two projects Crystal completed in social science, one in which she was required to do research on the topic of exploration and expansion. Crystal wrote a journal in the first person about what it was like to be on one of the first exploratory missions to the Americas. Another research project involved creating a video on the holocaust; for this Crystal wrote a play.

Crystal was a superstar in gifted-talented classes. She devised many unique and creative independent projects. She liked being able to decide what she was going to study. She was the leader of several group projects according to her teacher. She would stay after school and work on projects and come in on some Saturdays to work. With several other students, she started a school literary magazine. In the eighth grade Crystal had a few mid-quarter reports that reflected missing assignments, but she brought the grades up before the end of the quarter. Her mother was always at parent-teacher conferences, and during the seventh and eighth grades had several meetings with teachers about Crystal's problems.

Crystal's gifted-talented teachers saw her as a willing but very shy, quiet child. The gifted-talented program goals at the elementary level delineated in the Individual Education Plan (IEP) are broad and deal with expanding of math concepts, the analyzing of sentence patterns to produce original work, the exploring of the scientific method and mathematical relationships, the expressing of ideas and opinions creatively, and the developing of critical problem solving and creative thinking. Her seventh and eighth grade IEP reflected Crystal's strong interest in creative writing and language.

By the middle school level much of the gifted-talented programming was individualized, so Crystal had an abundance of opportunities to use her creative talents. She completed some exceptional products. According to her gifted-talented teacher she designed an exceptional public service announcement on environmental pollution. In eighth grade she also made a video yearbook. Her sensitivity to moods and feelings, along with her exceptional writing and musical ability, made her an outstanding video producer. However, even though a student may be extremely gifted, the gifted program did not provide any services for high school students; so Crystal had to leave the program. In high school, she therefore had no opportunity to excel at the things she loved best.

Future Education for Crystal

At the time of the interview, Crystal was still enrolled in correspondence school. She was doing well and accumulating credits needed for high school graduation. Her mother wished she had the answer to Crystal's educational problems. She was disappointed for Crystal. She was afraid that Crystal was going to look back and regret missing high school and wish she had done it differently. Her mother said she wished Crystal didn't have to get hurt to learn.

Crystal and her middle school gifted-talented teacher were looking into performing arts schools. Crystal was excited about this prospect. She did not want to stop being educated, just to be educated in a different way. As Crystal concluded below, we need to understand gifted students to help them succeed.

> That black sunshine
> In this pale grey sky
> Is the reason
> I no longer cry
> It calms my soul and
> Soothes my mind with
> The promise of death and
> The end of all time
> In the rays of Darkness
> I shall Hide all my sorrows and
> Pray to the devil

There will be no
Tomorrows
Please understand me
You never really did
Understand me
You always tried
But never quite got
It right
I'm not blaming you for this

Crystal kept going out with GIs and eventually became pregnant by one, who was later transferred to Saudi Arabia.

She and her biracial baby daughter live at home with her mother. Crystal and the baby's father enrolled in the district's "Options Program" designed for teen parents. She graduated in May, 1991.

DANNY, A DEAF STUDENT AT RISK

National attention is focused on the growing numbers of young people who are at risk of dropping out of school because of delinquency, pregnancy, drugs, and emotional illness. At-risk children who are also deaf have additional communication problems that further endanger their chances of completing school.

In our efforts to help deaf youth overcome their problems, have we unwittingly put students with learning and behavior problems at even greater risk? To examine this question, let's look at Danny, a 16-year-old tenth-grader who became deaf at thirteen months of age due to meningitis and who has profound sensorineural hearing loss in both ears.

A Handsome Young Man

When Danny, a handsome young man of average build, first arrived at the residential school for deaf children, his wavy, brown hair fell below his shoulders, an earring glistened in his ear, and the word fuck was tattooed on his left arm.

School officials told Danny he couldn't wear an earring at school. When he began riding the school bus, he argued with staff about the earring but eventually complied with the rule since none of the other boys at school wore one. He said he swallowed his pride and cut his hair above the collar because his father wanted him to cut it when he came to school.

Danny's parents were told they needed to investigate having the tattoo removed from his arm before he entered school. However, his father said they could not afford it, and Danny was allowed to enroll provided he wore long-sleeved shirts. Within a short time, Danny had his sleeves rolled up at every opportunity. Months later, after many warnings to keep the tattoo covered, Danny decided to black it out with a marking pen.

A Loner

Referral records described Danny as a loner, someone who kept to himself and needed prodding to work. At the residential school, Danny said he had many friends. He generally hung around several other students in the lunch room, in the student union, in the dormitory, and around campus. When Danny went home for the weekends, he said he went out with his friends, most of whom were older than him. Some of his friends were deaf, but most were not. They got together to play the guitar, dance, smoke pot, drink beer, and have a good time. Danny was variously described by students and staff as bad, defiant, both a leader and a follower, and charming. Even though he was often in trouble, he was very personable and likable.

Psychological Evaluation

Before entering the school for the deaf, Danny was evaluated by a psychologist. He was very cooperative and friendly. He communicated with the psychologist using sign language and talked openly about fighting, getting in trouble with the police, and using drugs. He appeared to enjoy working on various test items, and although he was easily discouraged, he persevered.

The Test of Non-Verbal Intelligence and the performance section of the Wechsler Intelligence Scale for Children-Revised (WISC-R) were given to Danny. His scores placed him in the average to low-average range of intellectual functioning as compared to norms for hearing and deaf children his age. During the picture arrangement subtest, Danny arranged the cards of the burglar breaking into a house and volunteered the information that he was "the same" himself. He then related his encounter with the police while breaking into a church.

The results from the Developmental Test of Visual Motor Integration and the Bender-Gestalt Test indicated that Danny might be experiencing a delay in perceptual motor development. Emotional indicators on the Bender-Gestalt revealed impulsivity and a lack of interest or attention to a task. This indicator is generally found in children who are preoccupied with their problems or who are avoiding doing what they are required to do. The evaluator surmised that this might indicate impulsivity and oppositional behavior on Danny's part.

The Piers-Harris scale results indicated Danny had low self-esteem. He scored high in anxiety, much lower in popularity, intellectual development and school status, and lowest in behavior. These results suggest that Danny believed he had a behavior problem, but nothing was causing him anxiety. He admitted his behavior got him into trouble, but that fact did not seem to bother him. Later in the interview, Danny revealed that he did feel upset and frustrated with himself.

On the Wide Range Achievement Test and the reading comprehension section of the Peabody Achievement Test, Danny scored between second- and third-grade levels in reading and math. His results for the Stanford Achievement Test (for hearing-impaired students) were the same. Given his intellectual ability, Danny should have been able to perform better in academics. Although he attended school with great regularity, once he became a residential student he received C in English, F in reading, and D in math. He received one other D and F. His best performance was in art and prevocational classes, in which he made Bs. Danny reported that he made good grades and was a good student. He said that he wanted to go to college and to get a good job in some field of science or in welding. He said his favorite subjects were plants, music, traveling, and drawing, and that he also liked to study, read, and work on the computer.

Danny at School

From classroom work and observations, teachers reported that Danny was intelligent, capable of learning, and likable. However, he showed weaknesses in areas of organization, study habits, concentration, writing, vocabulary, reading, language, math facts, attitude, and effort. Although Danny's teachers and principal were positive about him, the afternoon and evening staff painted a different picture. They had experienced multiple problems with Danny during unstructured hours. As long as he got what he wanted, things went well, they said. If staff tried to make him follow the rules, however, he argued, threatened, and blew up.

Danny at Home

Danny reported that he did not get along well with his parents. When not in the residential school, Danny lived with his father, two older brothers (one who was recently in prison), his stepmother, her daughter, and the daughter's two small children. Their home had four bedrooms, a kitchen, and one bathroom. Danny and his parents avoided each other as much as possible when he was at home. His father stated that he and his wife had their own entrances into their bedroom (formerly the garage) and that they basically stayed to themselves. Danny said that he had no duties around the house; his father didn't want him to help.

Danny's father, a 63-year-old veteran, had had to quit work because of tuberculosis. At the time of the interview he was disabled, visually impaired, and had heart trouble. Danny's stepmother seemed concerned about him. Neither parent abused alcohol, and they attended church often. Danny said his father was dirty and fought with his wife.

Family fights erupted occasionally, and Danny's older brothers beat him up when he got too far out of line. Danny admitted hitting his father on occasion. The father's basic attitude toward Danny's involvement in drugs, drinking, and sexual activity was that boys would be boys. He said someone ought to help Danny, but he felt powerless to do anything himself. Both parents had been minimally involved with planning Danny's school program and discipline procedures.

Danny with other Students

Danny's relationships with other students varied. He appeared "tough or cool" to some of the younger girls and boys, and they were both shocked and fascinated with his tattoo. Staff had confiscated crude love notes to Danny. He was rarely seen in the company of girls his own age. Younger boys seemed to admire him, almost to the point of hero worship. Older students who did not want to get in trouble avoided Danny. He came to school with a history of substance abuse, and he liked to portray that image. On one occasion he was caught sniffing the powder from an antibiotic capsule, and on another occasion he was caught sniffing correction fluid.

Danny could be very helpful and a leader. He often assisted younger boys in Scouting tasks. When some of the weaker boys fell behind, he carried their packs as well as his own. He had the ability to influence and control other students in the classroom. Yet, at other times, Danny had been observed doing what younger boys told him to do. In one incident, three younger boys decided to run away and invited Danny to join them. They hid in a barn for several hours before deciding to return to school. Danny often did not see the responsibility or consequences of his actions. Instead he appeared to observe a social power structure within the school.

Danny liked to hang out during unscheduled hours. He did not join recreational activities or participate in organized sports. He enjoyed walking to the nearby convenience store and going to the student union with several other boys.

Aggressive Behavior

Danny had a history of aggressive behavior, juvenile delinquency, and expulsions from schools. He had attended programs for hearing-impaired children in three public schools before being expelled and accepted in the residential program for hearing-impaired. Danny admitted he was always getting in trouble for fighting and stealing. While in public schools, he was often beat up by other students until he was about twelve years old, he said. He then decided he would be the aggressor. Danny had few communication skills and often lost his temper before he actually knew all the information.

At the residential school Danny was viewed as both a leader and a follower by teachers and other students. He often influenced other boys to get into fights and into trouble with adults and the law. In one dormitory incident, Danny persuaded another boy to steal a key from the houseparent's desk and to steal the boys' allowances. The two boys then divided up the money with other younger boys while on a Scout camping trip. During that trip, the two boys broke the door to the Scout canteen, planning to steal candy and other items. When the boys were caught, Danny was unafraid of the consequences of his actions. He showed no remorse about paying for the damages, going before the school discipline committee, being suspended, or having to face his parole officer upon his return home. In fact, when the superintendent accompanied him to his dorm room to watch him pack, Danny patted the superintendent on the back as if to say, "Don't worry. Everything will be OK. I'll be back."

In another incident, the deaf Scouts were camping in a public park. Two young boys on bicycles were curious about the deaf boys and rode close to their camp several times. The Scoutmaster caught Danny plotting an ambush in which he directed the other Scouts to surround and jump the two boys as they rode near the camp. Later, Danny directed the Scouts to peek into the women's showers.

Besides breaking into the Scout canteen, Danny broke into a church during the summer and was placed in a juvenile shelter. He ran away from the shelter and was gone for four days. Upon his return to school in the fall, he was still on probation. Even though he had violated his parole and was supposed to go back through the court system when he was later suspended from school, Danny went unpunished. What he did get was a four-week vacation. During the interview Danny stated that in general he does not get punished or restricted. He related that the only time he was ever really restricted or punished was by his father when he stole a car at about age thirteen.

Danny was also suspended for physical and verbal abuse of a staff member and chronic misbehavior. Thirteen incident reports were filed within the first two months of the last school year for the following incidents:

- attempted group rape of another boy for a joke
- refusal to study
- "mooning" young black males on a bus trip
- obscene gestures and language to staff
- refusal to remove his earring upon return to school
- bringing tobacco to campus and giving it to other boys
- refusing to do his dorm duties
- arguing, disrespectful, uncooperative behavior with staff
- attempted anal sex with another boy
- vandalizing dormitory furniture (threw and broke)
- disobeying dorm rules and fighting in the dorm
- physical and verbal abuse of staff
- damaging wall in dorm room
- stealing money from the dorm
- breaking into Scout canteen

Danny received other forms of discipline, such as work details, restriction to campus, restriction to the dormitory area, restriction to his room, supervised in-house suspension, suspension from the school bus, suspension for one and two weeks — along with counseling with the psychologist, the dean of students, and the principal. While discussing his chronic misbe-

112

havior with the dean, Danny commented that he didn't care, that the rules were too strict and "not good for you." He also refused to keep his tattoo covered as he was supposed to. The dean said Danny's attitude continued to be "one of absolute disdain for authority of any kind." For this particular referral, Danny was suspended for one week and his parole counselor apprised of the school's decision.

Danny stayed out of school an extra week. Upon his return, he wanted to attend a Scout training session, but he was not allowed to because he had missed the first session. Danny did not understand that he could attend the next time the training was offered. He began yelling at the staff, ran into his room, and slammed the door. He threw desks and chairs, cracking his bedroom wall. When the houseparents and supervisor entered his room, Danny assaulted them with karate kicks, then ran past them, yelling obscenities. Staff called for assistance from the superintendent, who stayed with Danny the rest of the evening.

Danny often fantasized or lied about the tattoo on his arm. When he first entered the school, he told the principal that his real mother put the tattoo on him. He told the psychologist and the dean that it happened when he was held in detention. In his recent interview, he related that he had gone to a motel with an older man. They were using drugs and drinking, and the man knocked him out. When he came to, the man had tattooed his arm.

Danny said that he used to be "smart-aleck," but that he was trying to control his quick temper. He said he didn't understand why he fought. In all the times Danny had been counseled or brought before the discipline committee, he only cried once, because he did not want to be suspended and sent home.

Five months into the school year and after continuous disregard for school rules, Danny was finally expelled for the rest of the school year.

The Role of the School

Staff members reported that Danny was a likable person in spite of all the trouble he had caused. He could be perfectly charming and exhibit good behavior one minute and become defiant the next. He didn't complete his school work, nor did he perform his dormitory duties consistently, yet everyone was willing to give him another chance. When Danny appeared before the discipline committee for striking staff and chronic misbehavior, he was told he would be suspended. It was the first time Danny ever indicated he was upset about punishment. He cried and promised to be good. He accepted the punishment and said he wanted to stay in school. Within the month, the discipline committee again had to suspend Danny. Two weeks after his return to school, he was expelled for the remainder of the semester.

After several unsuccessful attempts by the school to meet with Danny's parents and plan his school program, the high school principal, the language teacher, and the social worker met as a planning team to develop an Individual Educational Program, mandated by law for children who need special programming. Special plans were developed for reading, language, science, history, math, and speech. Classroom teachers indicated Danny was intelligent and capable of learning, but weak in academic areas and lacking in motivation and effort. Danny worked when he felt like working. He missed many weeks of instruction due to suspensions and the extra weeks he stayed at home.

Danny's instruction was individualized to meet his needs. As his reading level was very low, teachers made many materials to fit his level. Danny received hands-on experiences to facilitate his understanding of concepts. A variety of activities were provided to increase Danny's ability to concentrate. In addition, he was put in rotating classes, which gave him the opportunity to move from building to building.

Danny received individual counseling at school and was also scheduled to see the psychologist on Saturdays in his hometown. The counselor was also Danny's Scoutmaster, which enabled him to work with Danny in areas that Danny liked and excelled. Danny talked openly about his behavior, but he saw little reason to change. He had learned that the consequences of his misbehavior were not that bad, and that his charm might get him out of any punishment.

Although Danny did not get along well with dormitory staff, he appeared cool when facing the dean and other members of the discipline committee. The loss of temper, outbursts, and insulting language were never witnessed first-hand by the committee. Even during the superintendent's questioning of Danny and the Scouts regarding the theft of dormitory allowances and the breaking into the Scout canteen, Danny joined the discussion — explaining, reminding others how things happened, and freely admitting he instigated the activities. He was clearly the center of attention.

How do we help a boy like Danny? His parents said they felt helpless in controlling his activities at home. The juvenile system threatened Danny with punishment, but did not follow through. And the school was just that — a school. It planned special programming for Danny's educational needs; it provided counseling, supervision, structured activities; it provided social services that connected the home with other agencies for Danny's benefit. But, as a school, it had few sanctions to help Danny improve his behavior. Restrictions, suspensions, and even expulsions were relatively mild punishments for a young man who had learned to manipulate school authorities and juvenile court systems.

If Danny reapplied for admission to the school the next fall, he would most likely be accepted. I kept hoping that time and events between now and then would not wipe away those few tears that Danny allowed himself to shed — tears that revealed his innermost desire to control himself and stay in school. Too many chances taken in the past influenced Danny to take one more; but his tears seemed to cry out, "Someone please stop me!"

■■■

After Danny was expelled, he was caught selling drugs. Charges were brought against him, then dropped, then reinstated, then dropped again. When the police finally decided to follow through with their case against Danny, the district attorney refused to pursue it. Even after several other drug-related offenses, the judge refused to certify Danny as an adult. He was placed in DHS (Department of Human Services) custody and stayed in several children's shelters for awhile before being placed with a brother who was an ex-convict. A vocational rehabilitation center (a department of DHS) evaluated Danny for vocational training (to work on his general equivalency diploma and job training), but rejected him because of his inability to accept responsibility, his immaturity, and his continued use of drugs and alcohol.

Danny was arrested for burglary just before he "aged out." The courts couldn't decide what to do with him and finally sentenced him to three month's probation. He now lives with a second brother, also an ex-con. His social worker closed his case in December, when Danny became 18. He is now unemployed and receiving social security benefits. He has expressed no interest in attending vocational training and since he is now "of age" he can no longer be forced into such a program.

DAVID, A SOMETIMER

David at School

As the bell rang, David quickly got up from his desk at the back of the room. He gathered his books, and headed for the crowded corridors of the sprawling mid-Atlantic middle school. He ambled through the halls, greeting other students and often patting them on the back or nudging them. He made the most of this time between classes, entered his next class well behind his peers, and chose a seat in the back of the room. He sat quietly and rarely volunteered any information, but when called on he would respond. He appeared disengaged from the classroom environment.

David was 14 years old. He looked short for his age, about five feet two inches tall, and overweight at 140 pounds. He had fair skin, blue eyes, and shoulder-length hair tied in a pony tail. He often smiled and talked with students and adults in an open and pleasant manner.

Both the high school principal and guidance counselor identified David as a child with at-risk characteristics. His family moved frequently. He had attended a different school almost every year. His mother had been abused by several different men who had lived in David's home. He had repeated at least one grade and had been involved in a crime serious enough to warrant a referral to the juvenile court. His school attendance and academic records were poor. He seemed to be marking time in school.

Teachers reported they were unable to reach David. One said, "We felt helpless by the end of the year. We worked harder with David than I've ever seen a group of teachers work, yet there was no progress. He was in control."

David consistently tested at or above grade level on standardized tests of achievement. An individual assessment of his intellectual abilities revealed no learning disability that might account for his poor academic performance.

David's school records showed that the school systems in which he had been enrolled had spent considerable time and energy providing special services for him. They tried to interest him in school and to help him become a more successful student, but they failed. David still got Ds and Fs in all his academic courses.

One of his current teachers observed that David's case illustrated the need to extend vocational education into middle school. The teacher thought if David was involved with subject matter more closely linked to his particular interests he might be more motivated to learn. The teacher thought David was really interested in working and would be happy to find a job that wouldn't require any further education. He was not afraid of hard work, and waiting until high school for programs that engaged his interest was waiting too long. The teacher suggested that the system should redefine its values to meet the values of certain individual children posing problems such as David's.

The school David attended opened in 1974. It was a spacious one-story building located on approximately 50 acres of land. It had many educational facilities, including an industrial arts area, a library, and a large gym. The classrooms were light and airy, and all had windows looking out over the rolling countryside. Students attending the school came from five different elementary schools. All students rode buses to school, some from a long distance. David transferred to this school in November of his sixth-grade year.

Each grade level had space in a separate area of the school. The cluster of seventh-grade classrooms contained 108 students who were divided among three teachers, assisted by an additional gym teacher, home economics teacher, and industrial arts teacher. For the most part, classes were small. Teachers reported that their teaching situation had never been better and thought they were able to reach their students more successfully as a result of the improved student-teacher ratio.

The school day began at 8:50 a.m., when the students left their buses, entered the building, and headed directly toward their lockers in the wing where their classes were located. The students had 10 minutes to talk in the halls before going to their home rooms at 9:04 a.m. Classes began at 9:13 a.m. There were seven periods, each 43 minutes long. A half-hour lunch break for the seventh-graders came during the fourth period. The classes were heterogeneously grouped, except for mathematics, when David worked in the high group.

All of David's classes were small. With the exception of gym, a combined class with two teachers, the classes contained fewer than 15 students. Classrooms were bright, cheerful, and well maintained. All classrooms posted lists of the daily schedule of classes and samples of current student work. Homework assignments were clearly written on chalkboards. Most teachers followed similar routines. They usually began lessons with a review of the previous night's homework, introduced new concepts, then assigned work to be completed in class. The students worked quietly at their seats as teachers moved around the room providing individual help.

David's school was orderly. Students walked through the halls purposefully, talking and greeting one another on their way to their lockers or to class. The teachers and the principal were in the halls when students passed, and there was a sense of well-maintained control throughout the school. The teachers seemed to know their students well and enjoyed working with them.

David had been out with the flu the day before I visited the school. Although he had not done any of the homework assignments for any of his classes, he did not seem upset. He just shrugged when teachers reprimanded him for being unprepared. It seemed almost as if David and his teachers had mutually agreed that this was David's standard pattern of work and that little more would be expected of him. One of the teachers said, "David can't interact in class because he doesn't have the work done. He can never participate in small-group work in class for the same reason. You can't put him with a partner because he'll let the other person do all the work."

On the day I visited, David went to a first-period special study skills class with only 10 students. Then he went to a home economics class, and then to gym, where the students were taking a test on health and fitness. Because David had been absent, he was given time to read the book before he was tested. David's gym teacher told me: "David's a sometimer; sometimes he's involved in what we're doing and sometimes he's not."

When the students ran laps around the gym, David was one of the slowest in the group, and only halfheartedly participated in the sit-ups at the end of the class.

Following gym class, David returned to his homeroom for language arts, again isolating himself from the rest of the class and telling the teacher he hadn't completed his work. At lunch time, David ate in a separate detention room next to the cafeteria because he had not dressed for gym. The students then received an additional break for an outdoor recess after lunch, but David stayed inside because he had not completed a history assignment. The next period was math, where David was placed in the higher level of the seventh-grade math. He seemed interested in the class discussion, volunteering for the first time during the day and asking the teacher about some geometry problems. After about 15 minutes, however, his attention waned, and he began to rub his eyes and stare out the window. By 1:30 p.m. he had fallen asleep at his desk.

When classes changed again at 1:47 p.m., David woke up and walked to his locker. On the way he exchanged notes with a girl and then moved briskly through the halls to the industrial arts classroom, where the teacher was demonstrating welding. David appeared interested but he did not volunteer to take part in the class discussion. The next day, students were going to have a chance to try the procedure on their own. David was enthusiastic about this and turned to talk to the student next to him about the proposed project.

Classes changed again, and David cheerfully strolled through the halls to his locker, where he retrieved his language arts notebook. He then took up his place in the back of the history classroom. Students spent the last period on independent seat work on a month-long unit on the Civil War. David did little work. He drew pictures in his notebook and seemed to be daydreaming.

The teacher came over to him several times and tried to help him with the project, but as soon as the teacher left, David drifted off again. Classes were over at 3:17 p.m., and after a final visit to his locker, David and the other students boarded the buses.

David's notebooks, schoolwork, and locker were disorganized, although he did have all the necessary textbooks and notebooks for each class. His handwriting was poor, but his math papers were fairly neat. Most of the time he seemed to write in sentence fragments and he rarely completed his assignments.

When asked about his attitude toward school, David said he went to school "to see my friends and girls." He also said he was learning math and welding in school and that he liked math but didn't like English. When I asked him what changes he would make in school, he said he would have no homework.

David went through the school day in a cheerful, yet detached manner. He avoided becoming involved in academic tasks without challenging the authority of the teachers. One of his teachers said David particularly liked lunch and gym. "David enjoys social interaction. He has a pleasing personality, and the other kids like him. He responds to discipline quickly and is not a discipline problem. He just exists. He's smart enough to know what's going on and avoids real confrontation with authority figures."

Another of his teachers said David's attitudes and needs were much the same in all areas, although he probably did his best work in math if he applied himself. "In math," the teacher said, "we assigned him to the top group as much for the role modeling as for pacing him at a level where he should perform." This change made little difference in David's work. He had done well on a recent reading test, but he had not done an assignment in math in nine weeks. David had regular assignments in all areas and didn't do them. In class, he'd pick up his book and work while the teacher was in the immediate vicinity. But as soon as the teacher walked away, David put the book down and just acted as if he was doing something. He rarely, if ever, disrupted class.

Because David had moved and changed school almost yearly, tracking down his records was complicated. It was possible to find them only as far back as the second grade (the grade he repeated); records for third grade were missing as well. Those records included summaries of the nationally normed SRA (Scholastic Research Associates) tests, report cards, and other narrative information. In the second grade David earned four Ds and three Cs in academic areas, with Ss in art and music. When he repeated second grade, his grades were better — mostly Gs (Good) and an O (Outstanding Achievement) in reading comprehension and math computation. By the fourth grade, those grades had slipped to Gs and Ss (Satisfactory), with an N (Needs Improvement) in spelling, and a U (Unsatisfactory) in health. In the fifth grade, David earned only two Gs, and the rest of his grades were Ss, with three Ns (in language arts, science, and health). Also, in the fifth grade David briefly played violin in the school orchestra, and his teacher noted he had the potential to play well "if only he would practice." At the end of the sixth grade, David received three Bs, two Cs, three Ds, and one F (in math, the subject that could potentially be his strongest). And at the end of the first semester of the seventh grade, David had one B+ (technical education), two Ds, and four Fs.

The report cards from his elementary school years showed that David failed to carry out responsibility for his work, that he didn't do his homework, and that he didn't use his time effectively. The teachers' comments all suggested that David was capable of good work when he tried, but that his efforts weren't consistent. Teachers said: "David needs to study for health tests and needs to complete projects. He could be doing much better at school" and "David is capable of excellent work but rushes and doesn't really apply himself daily!" In the sixth grade, most of his teachers noted he had not turned in his homework. Only his second-grade teacher said David was not well behaved in class, and comments about his behavior do not appear after this year.

David's SRA test scores for the second, fourth, and fifth grades were all above average: his composite score (reading, math, and language combined) in second grade was at the 84th percentile nationally; in the fourth grade it was at the 78th percentile; and in the fifth grade it had fallen to the 69th percentile. A similar decline in all the subsets occurred. The total math score, which was at the 94th percentile in the second grade had dropped to the 66th percentile in the fifth grade. These scores were consistent with the teachers' observations of David's performance, and were well above the national average (50th percentile) for these tests.

David's scores for a subset of the SRA designed to measure "educational ability" were at the 74th percentile in the second and fourth-grade years, and increased to the 89th percentile in fifth grade. This increase in David's educational ability contrasted with the decrease in his performance, and indicated that he was far more capable of learning than he was demonstrating in the classroom at this time. The gap between performance and ability was growing.

When David was in the fifth grade, he participated in an attempted break-in at a small business in a nearby town. While the details of the episode were unclear, David had had some contact with the police department concerning this event. He was referred to a psychologist for individual testing and personality assessment. The results of the WISC-R showed that he was "an intellectually capable young man." His verbal IQ was 107 and his performance IQ was 98, resulting in a full-scale IQ of 102. David's performance on the Bender Visual-Motor Gestalt Test was well within normal limits, and the psychologist concluded that there were "no indications of a learning disorder in this youngster's cognitive testing. Any academic difficulties that he may experience are not the result of cognitive limitations."

The report also included psychological assessments made on the basis of the Rorschach test, which indicated that David was a "fairly well developed young man who presents a relatively solid personality structure. David does not produce the projective protocol of an aggressive or dangerous youngster. He shows well-developed empathic ability and the capacity to relate well to others." However, the psychologist did observe that while David's responses on the Rorschach test showed a "potential for abrupt and impulsive acting out under stress, [yet] he showed no evidence of maliciousness or undue hostility in the testing situation. This is not a pre-psychopathic youngster." The report cautioned that it would be very important for David to have access to an appropriate adult male role model, "as the absence of the father and the antisocial position of the two older brothers has made it quite difficult for this youngster to develop a healthy masculine identity."

When I asked David's teachers about his attitude toward school, one of them responded, "He doesn't like work! He'll think of any way to get out of it. He's a real passive resister. It's like throwing a punch at a sponge; it bounces right off. He has average or above-average scores on standardized tests, and his intellectual ability is definitely average. He just doesn't choose to concentrate."

From all reports and observations, David chose not to do his work most of the time. Instead, he sat quietly at his desk waiting for the day to pass. As one of his sixth-grade teachers said, "He has a sense of humor and charm. I never felt his refusal to work was personal, but more like playing a game with the teachers to get a reaction."

Another teacher said David enjoyed being the class clown. "He likes to make the other kids laugh. He has a pleasing personality and the other kids like him." He added that David had few friends and most of them were from other low-income families.

One of David's former teachers added, "There's something extraordinary there. He'll come up and maintain personal contact with us. For example, he'll bump shoulders or touch in some way, wanting to make contact in a nonacademic way. He wants the attention and positive feedback of human relationships, but has no use for academics."

The school had tried many strategies to reach David and his family. His poor academic performance and attendance record concerned school faculty, who alerted social service personnel to possible problems in the home environment.

Teachers noted David's potential for leadership and hoped to capitalize on this characteristic when they proposed to arrange for him to attend a private military academy in a nearby town. In the winter of 1988, the guidance counselor, the principal, and the sixth-grade teachers spent much time with David and his mother, explaining they thought he had the potential for being a good student as well as a student leader. They set up a contract system that he could follow to complete his school work and to show the school he was serious about transferring to the military school. Unfortunately, David's mother thought the military school was a type of reform school and discouraged him from carrying through with his contractual agreement with the teachers. The plan was dropped, and David's teachers said he had showed little enthusiasm for school since that time.

Staff members at David's school were supportive and concerned about David's educational needs. They attempted to contact David's mother regularly, particularly because of his poor attendance record, and were involved with social service agencies when there were problems in the home. Because David seldom did his homework, he was placed in a special study skills class. This strategy was unsuccessful. The guidance counselor said, "He just went to class and refused to do anything."

In another attempt to motivate David, the school arranged for him to work with a tutor from the Job Training Partnership Act who would help him improve his mechanical skills. Unfortunately, this effort did not work out.

David at Home

David lived with his mother and his 12-year old sister in a trailer park. It was on an isolated dirt road running off a paved county road, deep in the woods of a rural area. Several miles away, there was a university town with many cultural amenities, but it was light-years away from David's experiences.

The trailer park was a collection of about 10 disheveled dwellings. Broken-down or abandoned cars surrounded the trailers, and several large dogs suspiciously prowled the area. Inside the trailer were a living-dining room, a kitchen area, and two bedrooms. The living room had a sofa, television, coffee table, and an extra chair; there was space for only two or three people to move around. The room was decorated with family pictures and several pots of plastic flowers. The small windows were clean and decorated with freshly pressed curtains, and the kitchen area was tidy.

David's mother had agreed to talk about David and welcomed me pleasantly. She told me that David had lost interest in school and wanted to work. She said that David had recently gained a great deal of weight, and that she had taken him to the adolescent obesity clinic of a nearby medical school for an evaluation. They had started him on a weight loss program.

She said David was frequently tired and attributed this to the weight gain. He was embarrassed about going to school without clothes that fit well. The school had purchased some pants for him in the fall, but they no longer fit. She talked about how David enjoyed working and that part of the reason he wanted to work was to buy himself new clothes.

David's mother was positive about the school's attempts to help David, and told me about visits and phone calls from school counselors and social workers over the years. She said she had not been to David's present school because of transportation problems. She also told me David had received all Fs on his November report card, and that she knew he could do better if he wanted to. She said several different times that she "wished the school could make David do better." When I asked her about David's earlier school experiences, she said she could not remember them.

The previous summer David had worked for a man who owned a garage. He wanted to go back to work for him, but the man said he wouldn't hire David back unless he got good grades. David stayed in school partly because he really wanted to get his worker's permit.

David's sister was home sick from school the day I visited. She was lying on the couch and joined in our conversation. She agreed that her brother wanted to leave school and go to work. She tried to help her mother remember the details of where they had lived previously.

I asked David's mother several times to give me suggestions for ways the school could better help him succeed. She said, "I really don't know. The thing that has motivated David the most is the promise of working." When I asked her about David's homework, she laughed and said that he always told her he did it in school — he never brought anything home to work on. His sister said she knew he had homework to do, but he just didn't do it. The school had called his mother from time to time about David's schoolwork, she said, but David's mother seemed unwilling to confront David with this issue. The conversation drifted off at this point, and David's mother seemed unable to focus any further on the issue of his academic needs.

There was no mention of David's father, either in school records or by David or his mother. In addition to his sister, David also had twin brothers, around 20 years old and living nearby. Both brothers had had serious encounters with the law, and one of them was now in jail on a murder charge.

While David's school behavior was compliant, his younger sister was extremely volatile and had severe behavioral problems in school. Workers from the school and protective services noted how close David was to his mother and the enormous influence she seemed to have on him. David's mother constantly threatened to move the family, which "kept David in a turmoil." His sixth-grade teachers also noted, "He has a great deal of respect for his mom. She exerts a tremendous amount of control over him — emotional, not authoritarian — and he wants to please her."

David's mother appeared to be in her early forties and projected a pleasant, if weary, demeanor. However, the school and outside social service agencies reported that the mother had a history of impulsive and irresponsible behavior. She had been involved with a series of abusive men and had been in and out of a local shelter for abused women several times in the past few years. The mother also had a history of alcohol abuse, and her violent behavior in the home had been linked to alcohol. Most recently, she had gone to the local shelter for abused women, taking the children with her, because her boyfriend threatened to kill her with a knife. A variety of outside agencies were involved with these episodes and worked with the mother to help her create some order in her life. Those agencies were also in contact with the school, trying to prevent another change of school for David.

Conclusion

The complexities of the problems presented by David's school performance were obvious. The solutions to those problems were much harder to come by. A variety of social service agencies were concerned and were attempting to provide help and direction for the family. Those efforts were coordinated with the school's considerable effort to create a supportive environment for David. In our final interview, David's guidance counselor said:

> The school has done just about everything it can for David. We're always allowing him a clean slate, a fresh start, trying to give him a second chance. He did exhibit a real desire to go to military school, but then, for whatever reasons, decided he didn't want to go, and dropped everything. There's a lack of a strong male figure in the home telling David that there are certain values in a society that he needs to live by and conform to. The mother is powerless unless she changes her life. David will buy into anything that comes along. He's so gullible. He'll undoubtedly go to vocational technology in high school, but he has to apply even to be accepted there. The state has just passed a law that high school attendance is compulsory until age 18, so David is going to be in the system, one way or another, for four more years.

David's academic, social, and emotional profile raised many issues associated with children at risk. David had had a disjointed educational experience. One of the most frustrating problems in this case was the decline in academic performance coupled with above-average intellectual ability. David's home situation was unstable. His passive demeanor, combined with his obvious loyalty to his mother, kept him from coping with family problems and further disruption. School and social personnel frequently discussed David's situation in an attempt to work out viable solutions to his problems. The staff at the school and David's mother reported his willingness to work, and vocational education was probably the key to providing future educational opportunities for him.

In the year following the initiation of this study, the home situation continued to be unstable. The school worked actively with social service agencies. David was still attending school, and hopefully would apply to, and be accepted by, an alternative education high school. In many ways, David was fortunate to be in this particular school, and school system, because schoolworkers were able to provide a variety of support services. The school guidance counselor was guardedly optimistic that the alternative high school would provide the structure and incentive for David to stay in school and would prepare him for a responsible job once he graduated.

■■■■■

David's weight gain was attributed to "endocrine problems." The clinic prescribed medication and continues to monitor him. He has lost some weight and his activity level has increased. The school system has assumed responsibility for his continued evaluation and subsequent care.

Last year David's mother sold the trailer for $1,000 and took the family to Florida. When she ran out of money they returned to the area and lived with the Salvation Army for six months. David's sister suffered emotional problems after the move and became a ward of the city. She now lives in a detention home.

David attends the county's alternative high school. Recently he testified to the school board in favor of keeping the alternative school open. He is not a behavior problem, but he is not motivated and is not doing his work. School officials now think he should be in the county's technical (vocational) high school.

He and his mother live in the city in low-income housing. Schoolworkers are following him and still assisting him with his problems.